Praise for

The One Page Project Manager

The One Page Project Manager for IT Projects: *Communicate and Manage Any Project With a Single Sheet of Paper* is a remarkable resource for any business or IT professional who are designing and implementing IT projects. It is straightforward and easy to follow. Anyone who is practicing in the project management field will simply have to have this book.

> — Hossein Bidgoli
> Editor-in-Chief
> *The Handbook of Computer Networks, The Handbook of Information Security,* and *The Internet Encyclopedia*

This book provides important tools for the IT executive. Ineffective project execution is one of the primary causes of pain in IT departments, but over-engineering project management methodologies too often take on a life of their own. The One-Page technique has the optimal balance of ease-of-use, flexibility and simplicity that are the hallmarks of a tool that can be used by pragmatic, action-oriented IT teams. In addition to improving project execution, managing with these tools will make status updates and enterprise-wide communication a snap.

> — John Baschab
> Co-Author
> *The Executives Guide to Information Technology*
> Managing Director, Technisouce Management Services

If you've ever needed to manage several projects at once, you know the dilemma: there has to be a better way to track the projects quickly, concisely and reliably, but finding and learning that better way always seems too tedious, costly, or complicated. This book solves that problem.

> — Frank Luby
> Author
> *Manage for Profit, not for Market Share*
> Harvard Business School Press
> Partner, Simon-Kucher & Partners, Strategy and Marketing Consultants

This is the most productive method I've seen to capture the essence of project management. Not too complicated, not too simple. For those with experience this is certainly a method to adopt for rapid, vivid, and persistent communication. I wish I'd had this years ago, but am glad it came along now. It clearly saves time for an organization's key resources.

— Paul Germeraad, PhD
President of Intellectual Assets, Inc.
Instructor, Caltech

From Boise to Beijing Clark Campbell's *One Page Project Manager* has helped managers take complex tasks and reduce them to their most efficient core activities. If you are looking to maximize talent, time and dollars the *One Page Project Manager* is a MUST HAVE for your team.

— Chester Elton
Best-Selling Author
The Carrot Principle

When managing large projects it is easy to lose oneself in gritty details only to wakeup and realize that you spent valuable time on the wrong issues. In the *One-Page Project Manager,* Clark Campbell reveals a wonderful tool for keeping projects on task. Only one glance and we see the big issues requiring attention. It's the perfect organizational solution for the executive needing relevant project information.

— Taylor Randall, PhD
Professor, David Eccles School of Business
University of Utah

As you read through Clark Campbell's book, you will say to yourself, 'So simple, yet intuitive and useful; I can put this to work today!' IT projects require meticulous attention to balancing scope, time, and resources. And the most important factor in successfully maintaining this equilibrium is communication, which the *One-Page Project Manager* delivers. Use *The One-Page Project Manager* and your projects will better deliver tasks to your objectives and stay closer to timelines and budgets, while facilitating critical ownership and engagements.

— Todd Thompson
Former Senior Vice President and Chief Information Officer
JetBlue Airways

While at initial glance this book may appear to be simply about developing a "dashboard" for tracking an important project, it soon becomes clear that it is much more than that. The approach outlined by Clark Campbell, an experienced and accomplished project leader, provides a proven process for project management that significantly improves the chances that the project will be completed on time, on budget and on target for its intended purposes. Furthermore, it provides a straightforward yet compelling set of steps to ensure that those with the ability and responsibility to achieve the desired results are supported, guided and focused in their efforts to do so. This approach will prove especially beneficial to students and practitioners who want to learn and apply the skills and tools of effective project leadership.

> — Steven C. Wheelwright, PhD
> Baker Foundation Professor
> Senior Associate Dean
> Director of Publications Activities
> Harvard Business School

Impressive in its simplicity, yet universal in its application, the *One-Page Project Manager* began assisting Chinese project managers in 2003, when Mr. Campbell first lectured in Beijing. OPPM is easy to learn and use, and is impressive in its clear capacity to communicate. It should be required reading for every manager who wants to improve project performance, accurately tell their story, and do it efficiently.

> — Jonathan H. Du, PhD
> CEO and Chairman
> WiseChina Training Ltd.
> Beijing, China

THE ONE-PAGE PROJECT MANAGER FOR IT PROJECTS

COMMUNICATE AND MANAGE ANY PROJECT WITH A SINGLE SHEET OF PAPER

CLARK A. CAMPBELL

WILEY

John Wiley & Sons, Inc.

Published by John Wiley & Sons, Inc., Hoboken, New Jersey.
Published simultaneously in Canada.

For general information on our other products and services or for technical support, please contact our Customer Care Department within the United States at (800) 762-2974, outside the United States at (317) 572-3993 or fax (317) 572-4002.

Wiley also publishes its books in a variety of electronic formats. Some content that appears in print may not be available in electronic books. For more information about Wiley products, visit our web site at www.wiley.com.

Library of Congress Cataloging-in-Publication Data:

Campbell, Clark A., 1949-
  The one-page project manager for IT projects : communicate and manage any project with a single sheet of paper / Clark A. Campbell.
     p. cm.
  ISBN 978-0-470-27588-7 (pbk.)
     1. Information technology–Management. 2. Project management. I. Title. II. Title:
1-page project manager for IT projects.
  HD30.2.C3557 2008
  004.068'4–dc22

                                                                                      2008011984

Printed in the United States of America

10 9 8 7 6 5 4 3

CONTENTS

Clark Campbell has done it again . . . created another One-Page Project Manager (OPPM) winner! What would it be worth to you to insure that all of your Information Technology (IT) projects delivered their expected value? Clark describes a high-level methodology and tool to help you achieve this goal. Read on!

This book is specifically written for IT projects, which need all the help they can get because they generally have a poor track record of delivering expected value, as evinced by the following chart. The causes for these problems are twofold. First is *IT effectiveness:* the business and IT departments are seldom closely aligned

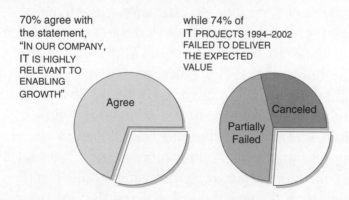

Even in companies that recognize the importance of IT, adequately fund IT, and actively seek to align IT with business goals, outcomes can be disappointing.

70% agree with the statement, "IN OUR COMPANY, IT IS HIGHLY RELEVANT TO ENABLING GROWTH"

Agree

while 74% of IT PROJECTS 1994–2002 FAILED TO DELIVER THE EXPECTED VALUE

Canceled

Partially Failed

Source: Bain annual management survey (*n* = 359), Bain Management tools survey.

and can judge project priorities quite differently. In other words, they are not operating as a singularly focused unit with effective governance. Second is *IT efficiency:* the IT organization is often inefficient and lacks agility in its development and deployment processes. When you put these two problems together, the results include a large percentage of IT projects that fail to deliver their expected results.

The OPPM for IT projects can help resolve these problems. In my experience, the OPPM for IT helps in three areas:

1. *Organizing the project:* Starting the project with a simple multidimensional OPPM that lets you see all the components of the project is extremely valuable. Project Objectives, Tasks, and Team Members are the beginning of establishing a successful project plan. The OPPM becomes the high-level plan that can be used with other detailed project management tools for day-to-day project execution. If a potential problem is not caught upstream, it is generally more costly to resolve in the project downstream.

2. *Establishing a common visual language:* One of the problems that causes disconnect between the business and IT is language. Although generally the business and IT speak the same national/cultural language, there is a business dialect and a technical dialect that are difficult to understand at times. Some people call it jargon. The OPPM is a visual representation of a common goal, the IT project. It is easily understood by both business and IT and has no jargon. It takes little, if any, training to understand

this common visual language used to improve communication.

3. *Improving IT and business alignment:* Using the OPPM as a project status communication tool (weekly or monthly) drives a tighter connection between the business and IT. This simple multidimensional tool is easily understood and offers a transparent view of IT to the business. The process of regularly using a common visual language to communicate project status effectively tightens alignment between IT and the business.

How do I know this? I have successfully used the OPPM in the last 10 years on a variety of different IT projects in three different companies. I have also experienced firsthand the described benefits. I have been a CIO for 30 years and have been responsible for the delivery of many projects. My most successful projects have been in the last 10 years using this OPPM methodology and tool. The method itself will not assure success. There are many variables that need to be managed to deliver a project that meets the expected value. However, I have found this tool to be very effective.

How would you know if this would work for you? Should you read the book and put OPPMs into practice in your IT organization? Let me tell you a little more about myself and my experiences to help answer this question. I started my professional career with IBM and spent 23 years in a variety of professional assignments. My last five years with IBM were spent as the divisional CIO of the General Products Division. Then, over the next 18 years, I served as CIO for six high-tech computer companies: Memorex, Unisys, MIPS, SUN Microsystems, Cirrus Logic, and Exabyte. In my last seven years, I served as CIO for O.C. Tanner. Why is all of this important? It is important because in my 30 years as a CIO, I have participated and directed hundreds of IT projects of all sizes and complexities. Many have realized their expected value, and some have not. I only wish that the OPPM had been developed and refined earlier.

To be candid, I think I have stepped, as it were, into and out of nearly every IT project "glue bucket." And, given the last years with OPPM, I would highly recommend the use of this tool in all IT projects. It is simple to use, easy to learn, and provides significant value to a project. The OPPM helps get a project going, creates a common visual language for communication, and effectively improves the IT business alignment. This is an innovative and simple tool that I consider a breakthrough for project management. If you need more motivation and/or help, give Clark a call and invite him to speak to your team and/or provide some on-site training.

Read the book and deploy OPPM is my recommendation. Good luck, and good reading!

DAVE BERG
dbergcio@yahoo.com

ACKNOWLEDGMENTS

Projects are, most of all, people dependent. A book about projects is certainly not dissimilar. And indeed, many people contributed in various ways to this book.

In over 80 years at the O. C. Tanner Company, the disciplines of project management emerged at various times, places, and under the leadership of Obert C. Tanner, Carolyn T. Irish, and O. Don Ostler. The genesis of the One-Page Project Manager (OPPM) was the coming together of three requests by CEO Kent Murdock. First, for all leaders to secure formal project management training; second, to codify a set of company specific project management methods; and third, to provide him with a simple, but not too simple, communication tool for projects large and small.

The initial OPPMs were designed by a team tasked to build a $10 million automated storage and retrieval facility. Wayne Carlston, Klaus Goeller, David Petersen, Dennis Smith, and I provided the basic ideas, which Byron Terry brought to life in Microsoft Excel. Once the form was designed and populated with data mined from the Primavera and the various Microsoft Project plans, David Petersen collaborated with all the stake-holders, filled in and aligned our progress, and prepared the very first periodic OPPM reports to management.

Could the OPPM be helpful in Information Technology (IT) projects specifically? Our original project (about which *The One-Page Project Manager,* was written) contained a modest $3 million IT component. This early indication that the OPPM might be IT useful was further sustained by more comprehensive IT projects guided by and communicated about using the OPPM. The collection of IT project successes and failures, coupled with a growing appreciation for and refinement of the OPPM are the backdrop for this new book. This was amplified by the remarkable demand for the first book. All of this is a collection of insight, contributions, and support from:

- The project teams that tackled Cornerstone, Entrada, ISO 9000, and a myriad of smaller IT projects.
- Byron Terry, Alan Horowitz, and Volkmar Nitz, whose fingerprints may be found throughout the book.
- The Project Management Office.
- Shannon Vargo, Deborah Schindlar, and the team at John Wiley & Sons.
- Operating Leaders, Management Team, and Professional Services Group at O. C. Tanner.
- Meredith, Mick, Tracy, Annie, Emma, Abe, Jane, Kate, Jarv, Jennie, Claire, Owen, Bennett, Peter, Genny, Lauren, Maren, Thane, Laina, and James.
- Marjorie and Asa; Edith and John.

Finally, gratitude is extended to a continually expanding group of companies and individual users and refiners of the OPPM.

Over more than a decade, the *One-Page Project Manager* (OPPM) grew from its fledgling ideas into a standard protocol within the confines of a single corporation. Now, with the first book exposed to the refining grist of the free market, it has found a unique and meaningful place in the discipline and profession of project management. I never could have forecast that OPPM would frequently be Amazon's #2 best-selling project management book just behind the *Project Management Book of Knowledge* (PMBOK), or that it would often be among the top 50 best selling of all management books.

This second book, *The One-Page Project Manager for IT Projects,* is in response to a growing number of inquiries concerning more specific guidance on how OPPM has in the past, and may in the future, be used specifically for IT related projects.

During the early years of project management's 40-year growth history, time lines and PERT scheduling techniques were the most commonly taught methods. Construction, engineering, defense, and aerospace were the drivers of more formal methods, with Primavera launching its project management tools in 1983. IT projects themselves began to be aggressively supported with the launch of Microsoft Project in 1990. Construction and IT projects possess both divergent and convergent requirements, broad similarities, and critical differences. Together, these have fueled much of innovation and creative development in the tools now available for today's project managers.

Einstein is reputed to have said, "Everything should be made as simple as possible, but no simpler." And with project management, the devil is certainly in the details. Project management has, of necessity, expanded its reach, its required learnings, its plethora of publications, and both its breadth and depth. Nothing illustrates this more than the PMBOK itself, connected to the reach and profound contributions of the Project Management Institute (PMI). A further manifestation is the massive functionality and expansive documentation for Microsoft Project, and Primavera, coupled with an army of training and consulting professionals ready to provide education and guidance through this complex network of knowledge.

How to communicate the complex simply—"that is the question." Dilbert posits an answer:

DILBERT: © Scott Adams/Dist. by United Feature Syndicate, Inc.

Edward Tufte is Professor Emeritus at Yale University where he taught courses in statistical evidence and information design. In his remarkable book, *The Visual Display of Quantitative Information*, he says, "Often the most effective way to describe, explore, and summarize a set of numbers—even a very large set—is to look at pictures of those numbers. Furthermore, of all methods for analyzing and communicating statistical information, well-designed data graphics are usually the simplest and at the same time the most powerful."

The 1848 Shaker song by Elder Joseph Brackett begins "Tis a gift to be simple, 'tis a gift to be free, 'tis a gift to come down where we ought to be." OPPM has proven to be a simple gift to those wrestling with project management communication, particularly for IT projects.

Remembering Einstein, it would only be a gift, if it was not too simple. The power and simplicity of OPPM is a combination of:

1. All five essential parts of a project (Tasks, Objectives, Time line, Cost, and Owners);
2. The linkages and alignment of each;
3. A clear, efficient, and accurate representation of both plan and performance;
4. An addition to, rather than a replacement of, current powerful project management tools; and finally
5. An intuitive picture that is easy to create and maintain.

Chapter 1 summarizes the content of my first book. You see how to construct and report using the One-Page Project Manager. If you are the CIO, Chapter 2 is specifically for you.

Selecting the right people for your project substantially raises your chances for success. Making those decisions poorly may doom the finest of plans. Chapter 3 presents some new ideas on the types of people essential to your project, and describes their assets, liabilities, and how to create a potent team.

The Project Management Office (PMO) can be found within the ranks of IT or it may be organized at the corporate level. Chapter 4 outlines how the OPPM supports the eight fundamental responsibilities of your PMO.

Chapters 5,6,7, and 8 provide specific examples of how OPPM was used to help plan, staff, direct, control, and communicate different IT projects. You will read about the launching of a dot-com business, the implementation of SAP, securing ISO 9000 certification, and the management of consultants.

Finally, Chapter 9 addresses some customizing ideas for OPPM—a little, but not too many.

Leonardo da Vinci said, "Simplicity is the ultimate sophistication." It has been suggested that OPPM may be the "da Vinci Code" for project management.

1

How To Construct a One-Page Project Manager

In my first book, *The One-Page Project Manager,* I covered in detail the thinking behind this valuable tool for project managers and how to construct one. In this book, I will be discussing how to apply the One-Page Project Manager (OPPM) specifically to information technology (IT) projects.

I first want to cover, in an abbreviated form, how to construct an OPPM. If you have read my first book, this chapter, which is based on that book, will provide a useful review. If you have not read that book, this will give you the basics so you can start applying the tool in your everyday work life.

THE THINKING BEHIND THE ONE-PAGE PROJECT MANAGER

Imagine your boss asking you to quickly provide a report on your project—what aspects of the project are on, ahead, or behind schedule; who is responsible for each of the project's major tasks; how the project is performing in terms of the budget; how well the project is meeting its objectives; what major problems have cropped up; and generally how well the project is presently progressing, coupled with a forecast for the next three months.

Wow, you think, that's a major undertaking. It will take me and my team hours to collect and organize that much information and put it into a presentable form. This could hurt our performance because this is time away from directly working on the project. And then there's a good chance the boss won't even read all of it because things are always hectic and the boss is always very, very busy.

After working on enough projects, I knew it was a challenge to provide upper management with the information it needed about a project, to provide it in a way that was easily understood and digested, and to collect and present the information in a format that did not take up too much of my time and my team's time.

This was the impetus behind the creation of the OPPM, which is a communication tool that I needed but that simply did not exist in the project management world. It is designed primarily to communicate all the most salient information a project's stakeholders need to know and provide it in a timely, easy-to-understand, and easy-to-compile format.

Moreover, every project has an important group of people deeply interested, though not directly involved in it, yet few project managers know how to effectively communicate to them.

This constituency may include the board of directors, senior management, suppliers, customers, and superiors or subordinates indirectly involved with the project or its outcome, and others. They want to be told what is going on in ways that engage them and doesn't waste their time, but they don't want to be given long reports with very detailed analyses. Yet, they also don't want communications that are too brief, too inconsequential, and too unsubstantial that tend to generate more questions than they answer. Instead, they want enough information to answer their questions, but not so much information as to cause them to become inundated with facts and figures.

The OPPM neatly balances their need to know with their desire to know just enough in an easy-to-read format. It answers more questions than it generates, which is why it is such an effective communication tool.

VISUAL ASPECTS OF THE ONE-PAGE PROJECT MANAGER

The OPPM uses symbols and color to paint a visual, easy-to-understand picture of where a project is at any given moment in time. And it links important components of a project. For example, managers of each part of a project are linked to their part in terms of deadlines and challenges. All stakeholders can easily see who is responsible for what, and how well each part of the project is going. Outstanding performance that exceeds the plan shows up and both management and peers immediately know who is personally responsible and who should be recognized. "Great management is born when recognition is added to the other characteristics of leadership." (See *The Carrot Principle* by Chester Elton and Adrian Gostick, New York: Free Press, 2007).

An aspect of a project that is going well is illustrated with a bright green box or filled-in dot. An aspect behind in terms of time, or over budget, is highlighted in bright red. When there is ambiguity, yellow is used. This use of color makes the OPPM visually clear and informative and allows senior management to quickly see what is going well, what is in trouble, and where there are some questions.

The layout of the OPPM also visually helps clarify the tool's information. Time lines, areas of responsibility, budget, tasks, and objectives are interrelated on the OPPM—just as in real life. The reader can quickly make connections between the important aspects of a project because of how the tool is graphically designed.

Let me make a statement here that may, at first, seem counterintuitive. Efficient, effective project management includes just the right number of details, while avoiding too many. Often, the more detailed and more elegant a plan is, the more pedantic and plodding the execution becomes. The details can become the drivers, and when this happens, you lose sight of what's important and the management process becomes ineffective.

One of the strengths of the OPPM—which can be counterintuitive—is having just the right degree of the *absence of precision*. For example, those deeply immersed in a project will want to know the status of critical equipment for the project—has it been manufactured, has it been shipped, where is it now, and similar concerns. But management only wants to know if it will arrive on time. The details of what it will take to make sure that critical equipment arrives on time are beyond the interests of management. They don't need to know that. This is an example of what I mean when I say the OPPM has an absence of precision; it doesn't cover every detail, nor should it.

Before I go into the specific steps involved in creating an OPPM, let me make clear one of its great strengths. It is a communication tool that can be used in almost every type of project. It may need to be tweaked when applied to different projects, but the basic tool remains surprisingly consistent.

Within IT, it can be used in a variety of projects, as I'll discuss later in this book. At the company where I work, O.C. Tanner in Salt Lake City, Utah, we've used it with such IT-related projects as implementing an enterprise-resource-planning software project, developing marketable software, launching a new Internet business, and obtaining ISO 9000 certification. Whatever your role in IT management, this tool can help you.

The OPPM navigates between failing to plan and over-planning. The plan is just the beginning, the means to the end, but not the end.

All of a project's owners are readily identifiable to everyone with the OPPM. Owners have no place to hide when a project is being monitored with this tool.

It makes clear—visually, through the use of interconnected graphics and color—who is responsible for what and how they are performing. Senior management sees, immediately, by glancing at one page, who is performing well and who is behind or having difficulty on their portion of the project.

Not only does this visualization make it easier for management to understand a project's status and who is responsible, but it is also an important motivator to the owners. They know that their role and performance is continually and immediately visible to senior management.

The OPPM is a tool that can be used in a surprisingly wide variety of projects. The OPPM evolved through several years and a number of projects to the tool that we now use. Originally, it was printed entirely in black and white; now, it has been expanded to use colors for the qualitative parts of a project and to highlight budget performance. These improvements have enhanced the tool's effectiveness.

FIVE ESSENTIAL PARTS OF A PROJECT— AND THE ONE-PAGE PROJECT MANAGER

The OPPM doesn't replace your existing tools; it augments what you are already using. The information presented isn't new. What's new is that existing information is placed in a format that is easy to use and to read. That's not a trivial distinction. By placing information in a new, easy-to-grasp format, management becomes better informed and those involved with the project become more highly motivated.

Every project has five essential elements (see Figure 1.1). It is not coincidental that the OPPM also has the same five elements; we have used the elements that make up all projects as the structure on which we build the OPPM. These elements are part of a project manager's DNA—they are second nature. The five elements are:

1. *Tasks: The how*—Tasks are the center of a project and need to be complete to accomplish the objectives. They are the nuts and bolts of a project, the specifics of what needs to be done—the work.
2. *Objectives: The what and the why*—Objectives are the vision, the where-you-are-going of a project. Objectives can be general or specific—the scope.
3. *Time line: The when*—The time line measures when things are supposed to be done and when they are actually done. Time lines can be elastic. If a project

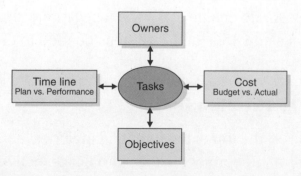

FIGURE 1.1   *Five Essential Elements of Every Project.*

is expanded, for example, the time line (and the budget) will probably have to be expanded.

4. *Cost: The how much*—Project expenses can have *hard* costs, like consulting and machinery, or *soft* costs, as with internal staff deployed on the project. Cost accounting can be complex, and every project needs input from accounting professionals.

5. *Owners: The who*—Task owners are the "who." This is vital. The OPPM makes clear to management who owns what tasks. Clear ownership makes obvious who deserves commendations for jobs well done and who needs to be assisted.

THE 12 STEPS TO CONSTRUCTING THE ONE-PAGE PROJECT MANAGER

The project's manager and the project's owners together build and maintain the OPPM—and then they live with it. Creating the OPPM and updating it must be a team effort. Owners own it. You, as the project manager, may have to negotiate with team members but, ultimately, you need their buy-in and full commitment. Figure 1.2 shows the OPPM template. A full set of OPPM forms is available for no charge at www.onepageprojectmanager. com. Let's now look at the 12 steps needed to create an OPPM.

Step 1: The Header

This goes at the top of the form and includes the project's name, project leader, project objective, and the current date.

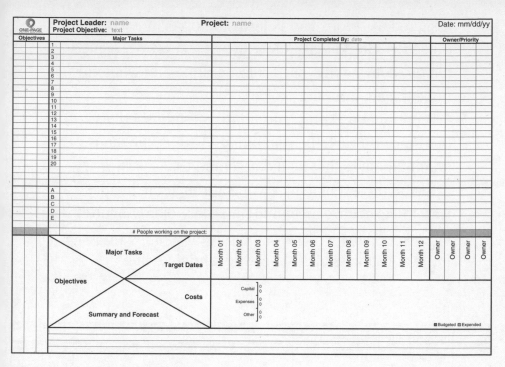

FIGURE 1.2   *Standard Template.*

Copyright O.C. Tanner 2007. **To customize this document, download it to your hard drive from the following web site: www.onepageprojectmanager.com.** The document can be opened, edited, and printed using Microsoft Excel or another popular spreadsheet application.

Naming a project is important because the name is what everyone will use to refer to the project from now until the project is finished—and even beyond. Consider holding off naming the project until the team is in place.

The project leader is the ultimate owner, and every project requires one, but only one leader. This person is almost invariably a full-time employee of the company, not a consultant or outside advisor.

The same people who give the project manager the project in the first place usually gives him or her the objective. If the project manager has not been given an objective, he or she must go back to those who assigned the project and clarify the objective. The objective should make clear: why those who assigned the project want the project to be done and what they hope to gain from the project.

A preliminary completion date is established at this time. Through the remaining 11 steps, the team's commitment to that final date emerges.

As the project manager works through the header with the executive assigning him the project (Figure 1.3), it is a good time to discuss the priorities of the project's triple constraints of costs, scope, and time line.

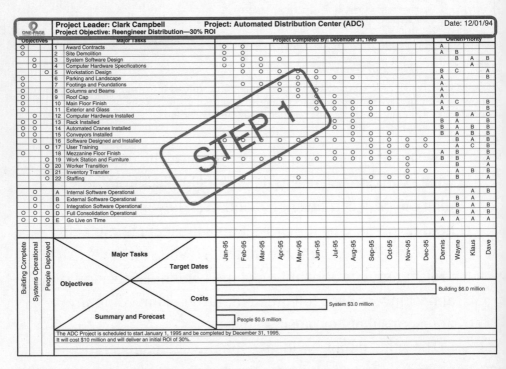

FIGURE 1.3 *The 12 Construction Steps—Step 1.*

The project manager will be making trade off decisions throughout the project. The key guiding principle will be management's ranking of these variables.

Step 2: The Owners

We'll assume from this point on that you are the project manager. Your next step is to name your team (Figure 1.4). These are the people who will manage the major components of the project. Your success, to a large degree, depends on them. They are the owners. Keep the number of owners as small as possible.

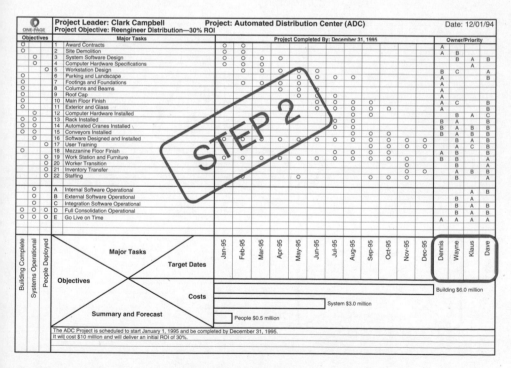

FIGURE 1.4   *The 12 Construction Steps—Step 2.*

From my experience, three or four is usually about right. On a large project, there will be more than one layer of OPPMs, and each will have its own set of owners.

Step 3: The Matrix—The Tool's Foundation

Think of the Matrix as the focal point, the hub of the project as expressed on the OPPM (Figure 1.5). Or, to use another metaphor, think of it as a compass that will guide your project from start to finish. The Matrix is the

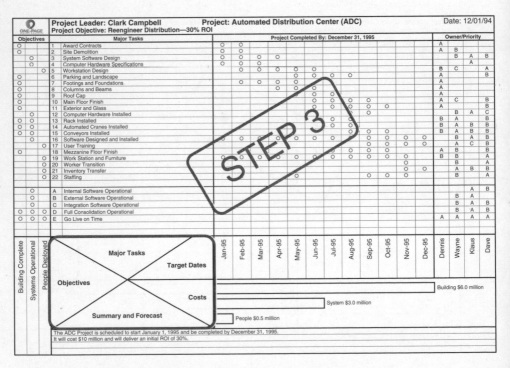

FIGURE 1.5   *The 12 Construction Steps—Step 3.*

OPPM's foundation. It links all of a project's essential elements and communicates them to your readers.

The Matrix flows naturally out of the creation of the entire OPPM. During this step, as project manager, you will want to present your team with an overview of the project, discuss how to handle the project, and go thoroughly through the pieces of the Matrix, including objectives, major project tasks, target dates, and budget. The Matrix is the focal point around which you will teach your team the fundamentals of the OPPM. Don't be surprised by the need to teach some of the basics of project management to your team.

Step 4: Project Objectives

With your team in place, you are now ready to break down the project into second-level objectives required to meet the main objective delineated in the header. Objectives go in the rectangle on the lower left-hand corner of the OPPM (Figure 1.6). Have no more than three or four objectives. With a $10 million distribution center project, we had three objectives: complete construction of the building; have the distribution center's systems operational; and hire, train, and deploy the people who will be running the center.

To set up objectives, ask yourself: how much time will be needed to complete the various objectives and what resources (financial, human, etc.) are necessary to meet the scope requirements and final deliverables. Later, as you outline the tasks, you will want a fairly equal distribution of tasks for each second-level objective.

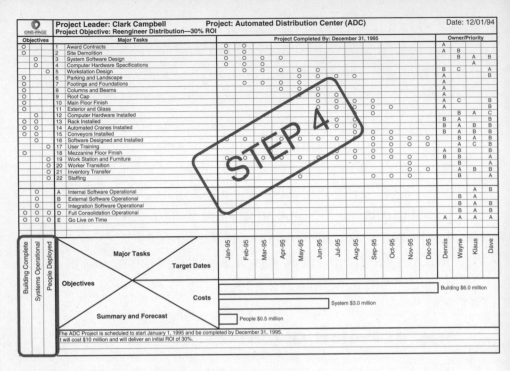

FIGURE 1.6 *The 12 Construction Steps—Step 4.*

Copyright O.C. Tanner 2007. **To customize this document, download it to your hard drive from the following web site: www.onepageprojectmanager.com.** The document can be opened, edited, and printed using Microsoft Excel or another popular spreadsheet application.

Step 5: Major Project Tasks

On the left side of the OPPM, we place the major project tasks (Figure 1.7). Large projects are really just the sum of many smaller projects that are coordinated and combined to add up to the final project. On the topmost level OPPM, each of these projects is expressed as a task, such as award contracts to subcontractors, design systems, lay the foundation for a building. Tasks should be measurable in terms of their progress so you can gauge their advancement and report on them in the OPPM.

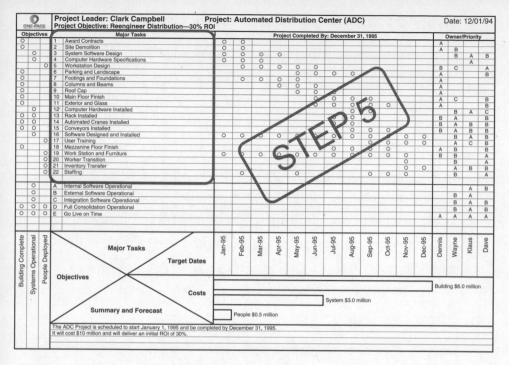

FIGURE 1.7   *The 12 Construction Steps—Step 5.*

Each task is assigned at least one owner, which is why getting the buy-in from team members for each task is essential. Match tasks with the strengths of the owners whenever possible.

Try to average two to three tasks per reporting period for the length of the project. If a project will run 12 months, 30 or so tasks are about right. Most projects are divided into monthly increments. Some tasks will be as short as one month, while others will last the full time line.

Keep in mind that behind each of these tasks, you could have another OPPM, or a *Microsoft Project* or *Primavera P3* PERT chart.

Step 6: Aligning Tasks with Objectives

In this step, make sure the tasks on your list will, when completed, produce the project's objectives. As you go through your tasks and objectives, it is essential the two match up. All tasks are aligned with at least one objective; some will naturally connect with more (Figure 1.8).

This alignment of task and objective often reveals inconsistencies or things missing. The process of alignment is not something done once and left forever. As you work your way through building the OPPM, with each step it is natural that you reevaluate preceding

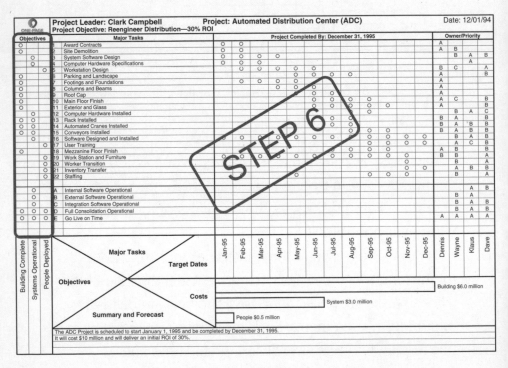

FIGURE 1.8   *The 12 Construction Steps—Step 6.*

steps and try to constantly improve. Identifying tasks may reveal a missing objective. You may also find a disproportionate number of tasks aligning with a single objective, therefore suggesting further evaluation of both.

This form of progressive elaboration will enhance the quality of your plan as well as the communicating power of your OPPM.

Step 7: Target Dates

The target dates are found in the rectangle running left to right near the bottom of the OPPM (Figure 1.9). Here we break down the time line into discrete steps, most

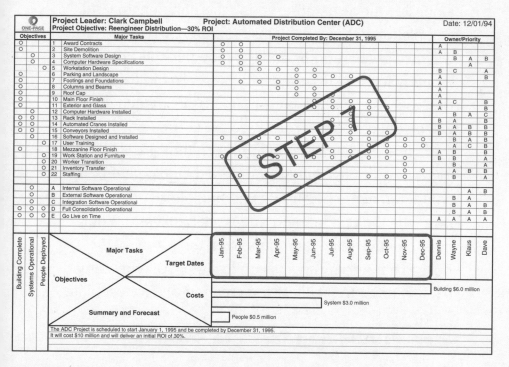

FIGURE 1.9   *The 12 Construction Steps—Step 7.*

commonly monthly (though a short project may have weekly or biweekly steps, and a very long project may have commensurately longer periods). Every period does not need to be the same length. Keep in mind that when you let everyone know the project's time line and time increments, you magnify your responsibility for meeting them. As with tasks, you need total buy-in for time from your team.

Step 8: Aligning Tasks to the Time Line

This step involves creating a time line for each of the project's tasks. We place an empty circle in the boxes alongside the task, representing the start, length, and completion date for each task (Figure 1.10). If the task will take seven months and the time buckets are in monthly increments, there will be seven circles next to this task. As each task is completed, the aligned circle will be filled in.

Each team member will approach the task time line discovery process with very different kinds of thinking. Some start at the beginning and think forward; some, start with the end in mind and work backward. Your most creative team members often think "out of the box" in a random way. It is critical that you encourage each in order to facilitate the creation of a robust plan.

Step 9: Aligning Tasks to Owners

Tasks have owners, usually one, rarely more than three. No matter how many owners per task, a priority between owners must be set. There is almost always *one* main

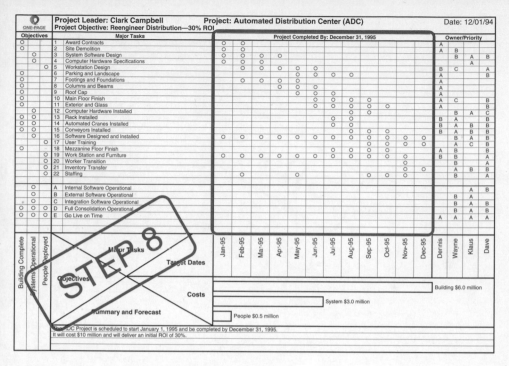

FIGURE 1.10   *The 12 Construction Steps—Step 8.*

Copyright O.C. Tanner 2007. **To customize this document, download it to your hard drive from the following web site: www.onepageprojectmanager.com.** The document can be opened, edited, and printed using Microsoft Excel or another popular spreadsheet application.

owner per task. The letter A on the OPPM designates that owner as the primary one (Figure 1.11). A subowner would be designated as a B owner, and someone subordinate to that owner would be a C owner. Who owns what is decided through a process of negotiation between team members, with you, as project manager, providing leadership and, if need be, mediation.

Step 10: Subjective Tasks

This is the portion of the OPPM that deals with subjective or qualitative tasks. Not everything about a project can

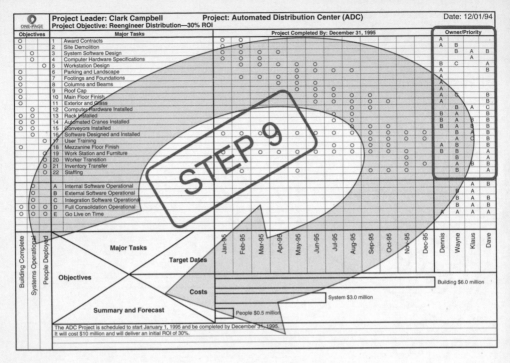

FIGURE 1.11   *The 12 Construction Steps—Step 9.*

Copyright O.C.Tanner 2007. **To customize this document, download it to your hard drive from the following web site: www.onepageprojectmanager.com.** The document can be opened, edited, and printed using Microsoft Excel or another popular spreadsheet application.

be quantified on a time line (software performance, for example). A computer programmer's sense of adequate performance may be quite different from an end-users. Think of cell phone service. A dropped call would be considered unacceptable, but what about sporadic static? Is that acceptable once in a while?

Situations like these are subjective. This section is where you place the subjective aspects of a project (Figure 1.12). Be sure, though, the objectives and owners are aligned with these subjective tasks just as they are with the more quantifiable tasks. Judgments concerning

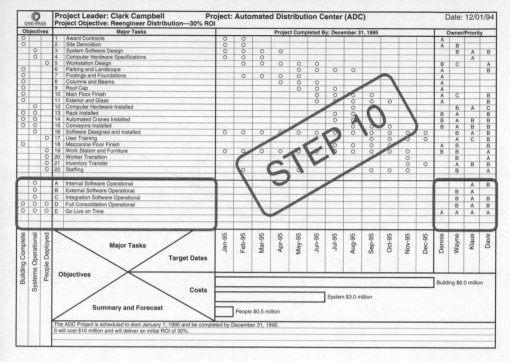

FIGURE 1.12   *The 12 Construction Steps—Step 10.*

Copyright O.C.Tanner 2007. **To customize this document, download it to your hard drive from the following web site: www.onepageprojectmanager.com.** The document can be opened, edited, and printed using Microsoft Excel or another popular spreadsheet application.

performance against these tasks will be shown as red, yellow, or green.

Step 11: Costs

On the lower right-hand side of the OPPM is where the budget is represented (Figure 1.13). The budget is dealt with simply, using bar graphs, with a bar graph for each portion of the budget. When the portion is on budget, it is depicted with green. When it is running over budget but is recoverable, it is shown in yellow. And when it is incurably over budget, it is depicted in red.

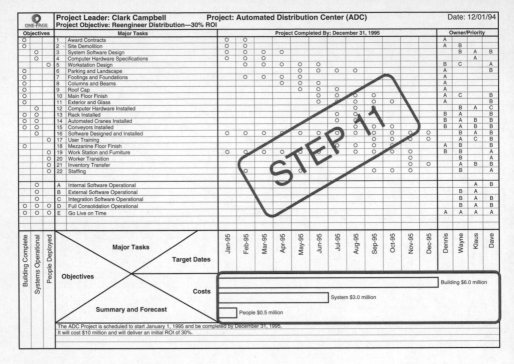

FIGURE 1.13   *The 12 Construction Steps—Step 11.*

Showing the budget on the OPPM is easy; deriving it is much more difficult. Before you draw up the budget, know all your costs. Include provisions for incremental increases, such as those due to uncertainty or potential changes in the project. This is the place to show contingency funds.

Step 12: Summary and Forecast

A good summary clears up any ambiguities or glaring questions, and heads off potential future misunderstandings. Everybody should now be "reading from the same page"—both literally and metaphorically. The summary is used to answer questions prompted by the graphics, not to explain the graphics themselves. Your language should add future expectations to your analyses—a what's next to the why. Here you will need to be as succinct and comprehensive as possible. The space for the summary and forecast is limited (Figure 1.14). This is by design. The lack of space forces you to be selective about what you describe and to be efficient in your discussion. Do not try to expand the summary space by attaching additional pages or diagrams. The power of the OPPM rests, in part, on the fact it is, well, one page.

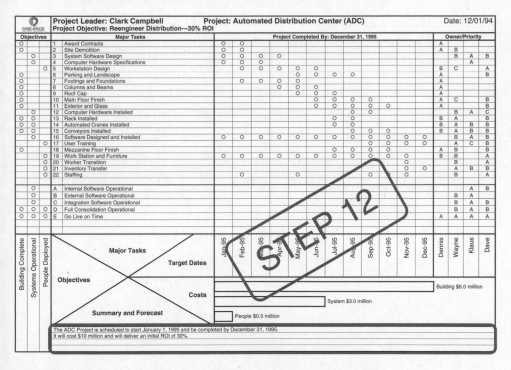

FIGURE 1.14   *The 12 Construction Steps—Step 12.*

FIVE STEPS TO CREATING A REPORT USING THE ONE-PAGE PROJECT MANAGER

Creating an OPPM report for each time period (usually monthly) involves five steps. You meet with your project's owners near the conclusion of each target date and complete the following tasks:

1. *Bold the target date.*
2. *Fill in major task progress.* This is where you fill in the dots. While filling in the dots is easy, getting agreement from team members on which to fill in or not fill in is often anything but easy. Your job as project manager is to bring the team together and communicate unambiguously.
3. *Designate qualitative performance.* This involves using colors. At O.C. Tanner, we define green as adequate performance, yellow as worrisome performance, and red as dangerous performance. As with filling in the dots, agreeing to the colors is essential, and can be a source of tension and require negotiation.
4. *Report expenditures.* Figures should come from the accounting department, which has to be in agreement with how the budget is portrayed on the OPPM.
5. *Write the summary and forecast.*

Figure 1.15 is an example of a completed OPPM 11 months into the 12-month project.

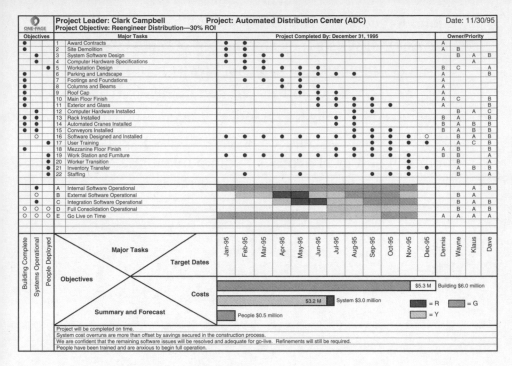

FIGURE 1.15   *The November ADC Report.*

You now have the basics of creating and using the OPPM. We'll spend the remainder of the book discussing how to apply the OPPM to IT related projects. The goal is to take what, to this point, has been a somewhat abstract discussion, and make it a practical, hands-on exercise.

One final comment: A November 2007 *Harvard Business Review* article asks, "Are Your Engineers Talking to One Another When They Should? . . . Cost overruns, schedule slippage, and quality problems often result from a failure to provide timely information. . . . It is important that teams are working with the optimum communication tools" ("Are Your Engineers Talking to One Another When They Should?" by Manuel E. Sosa, Steven D. Eppinger, and Craig M. Rowles). The authors propose a "compact and visual" communication tool designed specifically for project engineers. The OPPM is just such a compact and visual tool uniquely designed for the highest level of project communication. Please use and enjoy it!

Read This If You Are the CIO

This book is about applying the One-Page Project Manager (OPPM) to the information technology (IT) projects you assign or delegate, but as an executive director who oversees projects, you need to provide executive direction, and that includes having your team generate sufficient and efficient communication using the OPPM.

This chapter gives you:

1. Tips on getting the OPPM used in your organization, and
2. A quick understanding of the OPPM.

With this one chapter, you will learn how to read, understand, and interpret the tool to enable you to use it to best effect.

It would be best if you read this entire book, but if you do not want to, at least read this one chapter. As a leader, you don't need to know all the steps and details that go into creating and maintaining an OPPM, however, what you do need to know is what the OPPM is saying. You have to understand all the information it is conveying, and that's what I'll describe in this chapter.

TIPS TO ASSURE THE ONE-PAGE PROJECT MANAGER IS USED

Here are some tips that will help assure the OPPM is used effectively for all IT related projects:

- Be sure your project managers and team members understand the value of the tool. You can try to force your people to use the OPPM by making its use mandatory, but making team members willing believers is much more effective than coercion. When they understand how simple it is to use and how powerful and valuable it can be, they will naturally want to use it. But they first have to understand the tool's value. You may want to encourage them to read this book and review the free downloadable forms available at www.onepageprojectmanager.com. Having even one person in your organization become competent, confident, and conversant in the OPPM should be enough to get your entire organization behind it. That one person becomes the messenger, the advocate, and the champion throughout your organization. Experience has shown that once a project manager begins to use the OPPM, acceptance, enthusiasm, and even expectations follow. Project managers have often developed their own ideas and methodologies for project communication. As CIO, in the end, you may have to make using the OPPM a requirement.

- Make it clear that you and other upper-level managers prefer not to read long reports or insufficient summaries of projects, but will read OPPMs. This will encourage those working on projects to make the OPPM part of their communications toolkit as quickly as possible.

- Have a standard version of the OPPM in your organization. Discourage numerous versions to be developed because this will make the tool cumbersome and ineffective. Of course, different types of IT projects will require the OPPM to be tweaked to meet their needs. That's what this book is about. You should allow only relatively minor modifications to meet the needs of individual projects. I suggest as a template the one available on www. onepageprojectmanager.com, and shown in Figures 1.2 and 1.15. You want to keep things simple, so limit the variations of the OPPM used within your organization.

- Be sure the OPPM is used universally within your organization. If upper managers like you are not committed to its use, it will never be adapted or effectively used.

You benefit from the use of the OPPM because it:

- Dramatically reduces the time it will take you to review a project.

- Causes your project managers to improve the quality, timing, and cost effectiveness of their projects by making them review all the important parts of a project on a regular basis and by making the lines of responsibility clear.

- Makes clear to you certain salient pieces of information that traditional project summaries often obscure, such as who the owners of specific parts of a project are and where all the important parts of a project stand in terms of meeting their deadlines and budget.

- Reduces the time, manpower, and resources needed to convey important information about projects to upper management, giving project teams more time to spend doing what they really want to do, namely working on their projects.

- Uses graphics that visually display performance against scope, time, and costs.

- Will reduce and in some instances eliminate the need for formal project review meetings.

- Prompts the right questions.

- Depicts yesterday's vision, today's performance, and tomorrow's forecast.

HOW TO READ THE ONE-PAGE PROJECT MANAGER

The OPPM has several essential parts that are easily understood. In fact, you could probably look at the OPPM without any instruction and figure out most of its workings, it is that intuitive. But the brief descriptions that follow will help you understand some of the thinking behind each part. Refer to Figures 1.2 and 1.15 to show how the part fits in with the overall OPPM:

1. *The Header:* This is very basic, and includes the project's name, the project's leader, the project's objective, and the date of the report. At a glance, you see what the project is about, who is in charge, what the project is trying to accomplish. You and senior management complete this together with your project manager.

2. *The Owners:* This part tells you who is in charge (who owns) each part of the project. Responsibility is made public here. An "A" owner is the primary owner of that task, the one who is most responsible for seeing it through to completion. The RACI breakdown of ownership may also be used effectively with the OPPM. This will be discussed in detail in Chapter 5.

3. *The Matrix:* This is the heart of the OPPM. It is where various parts of the OPPM come together. Use it as a compass to point you to the pieces of information (objectives, major tasks, deadlines, budget, summary and forecast) you are interested in at that particular moment.

4. *Project Objectives:* These might also be called subobjectives because they are subordinate to the project's overall objective. Some suggestions here by you to your project manager might prove helpful in further clarifying your expectation simply shown in the header. This is a good place

to reinforce the SMART model for writing objectives (Specific, Measurable, Action-oriented, Realistic, Time-limited).

5. *Major Project Tasks:* This is arguably the most important component of the OPPM. Here you see the major tasks that need to be finished in order for the project to be completed. The numbered tasks are objective tasks, which are tasks that can be objectively measured. Subjective tasks, which are lettered, are tasks not lending themselves to objective measurement; they are qualitative rather than quantitative. The degree to which software is operational, for example, is difficult to measure. Is the screen format user-friendly, or adequately responsive? Such subjective tasks are placed in the lettered portion of the task section.

6. *Aligning Tasks with Objectives:* Here is an interpretative aspect to the OPPM. You look at the tasks and objectives with an eye to making sure the tasks listed will, when completed, produce the objectives you are aiming for. The circles tell you which objective (or objectives) is tied to which tasks. Part of the power of the OPPM is that it will show you how different parts of a project relate. In this case, we are using the tool to see how tasks and objectives work together. You really need to do this analysis only at the beginning of the project.

Once you are sure the tasks will lead to your objective, you will not need to visit this again, unless you change the project's objectives (which is actually fairly common). As a project progresses, you and your project team may reevaluate succeeding steps, similar in concept to continuous improvement in Total Quality Management. Some tasks may be aligned with two objectives, which is okay, but most tasks are aligned with just one objective, and all tasks must be aligned with at least one objective. If a task does not contribute to meeting one of the objectives, it should not be there.

You as the leader are looking for both context and balance here. For example, a project team with deep experience in one subobjective area will overload tasks aligned to their expertise, where tasks necessary to other less-experienced subobjectives may receive insufficient delineation.

7. *Target Dates:* This is where you can easily see how well each task is proceeding in terms of its time progression and deadline. The vertical line tells you where on the time line you are now. The time line is usually divided into months. However, the time units do not have to be months. Short projects may be divided into weekly increments while long ones into bimonthly or quarterly increments. Also, some projects may have different length buckets on a single time line. The dots (used with the objective tasks) indicate the months allotted for each task. When a dot is filled in, it is complete. If a task has dots not filled in and the vertical line is to the right of the dots, it indicates the task is behind schedule. Much has been studied and written about the time planning for IT projects. Being a CIO, you know that statistics show the longer a project, the higher

the rate of failure. As it turns out, the OPPM is well suited to facilitate "path-based" planning or project "chunking." An example of how I learned that the hard way is examined in Chapter 6.

We use color and a bar graph to depict subjective tasks. If a task is green, then performance is adequate, while yellow indicates performance is worrisome but solvable. Red indicates performance issues are seriously endangering cost, scope, or timing.

8. *Costs:* This is done as a bar graph representing the budget. The budget stands alone and is not graphically aligned to the time line. This graph provides a quick, easy-to-understand picture of where the budget is at any given moment.

9. *Summary and Forecast:* This small section of the OPPM is small for a reason—to make sure there are no lengthy explanations. It is where the project manager and project team address issues raised in the body of the report. It is not a place to restate the obvious, but a place to answer the questions posed by the graphics and communicate remedies and expectations for the near-term future.

A LITTLE MORE . . .

These are the basic parts of the OPPM. Let me make a few more comments about how to read and use this tool:

- *Pay attention to the colors.* Greens you expect, yellows are cause for concern, and reds really need your attention.

- *Pay attention to the dots.* Open circles to the left of the vertical line are cause for concern. The more empty dots to the left of a line associated with a given task, the more behind schedule is that task. And the more behind schedule, the more that task needs your—or someone in upper management's—attention.

- *Look at the budget line and make sure the project is running at or near budget.* If not, give the budget your attention. Find out from the project manager and the owners what the problems are. Yellows may be adequately addressed in the Summary and Forecast section. Reds prompt a face-to-face meeting in many organizations.

- *Pay attention to owners.* It is obvious that when an owner has several tasks in trouble, that owner has some explaining to do. Hold him or her accountable. But don't ignore the positive. An owner, who, during a project, consistently finishes tasks on or before schedule or on or under budget, should be appreciated. The OPPM helps hold people accountable, and when someone is performing well, they deserve positive recognition—as does their team. There is power in appreciation. "When recognition is applied to good management, it serves as an accelerator of employee performance and engagement." (*The Carrot Principle, 2007.*) These variables have been shown to magnify efforts to appreciate: 1. Enlarging the audience; 2. Embedding a cadence; and 3. Amplifying receptivity. OPPMs substantially assist in communicating exceptional project performance to a larger audience with a required cadence. They combine a standard methodology with a refined data integrity ensuring eager receptivity for the acknowledgement of great work.

- *Read the summary and forecast.* This is where you will learn the whys behind the information presented in the OPPM, and what your project team sees as the forecast of issue resolutions and future performance.

- *Understand that the OPPM does not provide you with all the details.* You can't see or understand the nitty-gritty going on with a project by reading the OPPM. The challenge that a certain task has meeting its deadline is usually not obvious on the OPPM (unless discussed in the summary and forecast). This absence of detail is on purpose. The OPPM is an effective communication tool for upper management precisely because it lacks great detail. You don't usually need to know all the details. The OPPM gives you the big picture, the broad strokes. That's the power and the beauty of the tool. If there is an aspect to a project you want to know more about, you can always ask the project manager or the project's owners. The OPPM highlights what is important to upper management, and leaves out the rest.

- Your project management office or chief project officer (CPO) could hold short monthly meetings with each project manager, review their OPPMs, and help determine which project requires your high level review and which would be helped by your personal involvement in a meeting.

Your Project Team: Who to Pick, How to Mix-and-Match

This chapter is based solely on my observations and no claim is made to any psychological, academic, or clinical expertise on my part. We have all read about right-brained versus left-brained predisposition, about multiple intelligence, and about IQ and EQ. My thoughts as a project manager are crafted into a simple, easy-to-understand-and-apply thinking model to assist in constructing your project team.

Before starting any project, the project leader is faced with what is often the most difficult decision concerning the entire endeavor: Who to put on the project team. Nothing is harder than identifying the right mix of people. It's like cooking: If your ingredients are poor, no matter how wonderful the recipe and how carefully you follow the instructions, the end result will be wanting. But get superior ingredients and mistakes and accidents can often be made up for.

The same thing holds true for project teams. I've spent a lot of time thinking about the types of people I want on my teams. And, yes, people come in different "types." I don't mean this in a denigrating way or that I stereotype people, such as the popular Type A and Type B personalities. But each of us has strengths and weaknesses. Albert Einstein was a great physicist, but that doesn't mean he was a wonderful athlete. Bill Gates is an innovative genius, but I doubt he is a great violinist. Michael Jordan could play basketball like no one else, but baseball was another matter.

After years of experience, scores of projects, and a fair amount of time thinking about the issue, I've identified three types of people who, when brought together, create an ideal mix for managing any type of project, and for our purposes here, specifically IT projects. Some people fit into two of these types (few have all three attributes). Figure 3.1 shows how these types can

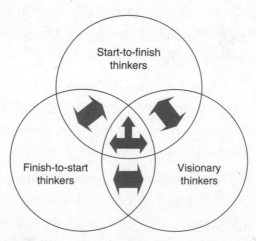

FIGURE 3.1   *Project Thinkers.*

overlap. They are the ingredients you need to help assure your project team is successful. When you have these types represented on your project team, you have all the strengths you need and the ability to override any notable weaknesses. Let's look at these three types.

THE VISIONARY THINKER

Visionaries are generally your brightest and most creative team members. They are out-of-the-box thinkers; they think about things in novel ways; they can dive deeply into a subject or think across a wide range of subjects. They're not encumbered with the structure of how things are. They turn things upside down, twist and turn them in new and unique combinations. The IT world enjoys a particular concentration of visionaries.

As a project manager, be aware that it is absolutely essential to have visionary thinkers on your team. They may sometimes create unique difficulties, but they amplify the deliverables of a project, and they enhance and augment a project's outcome.

They find solutions to intractable problems. They challenge conventional thinking and are less encumbered by "group think." You will often hear them say, "Why not ..." or "How about ..." I cannot imagine a robust project team without visionaries.

Even though innovative visionaries are essential to a strong project team, like every type of thinker, they come with unique challenges. The liability of visionaries is that they are not focused much on the commercialization or the actual completion of the work. Once they've completed thinking through a problem, they are on to the next thought. They generate lots of ideas, but others must implement them. So as you proceed forward on your project planning before the project actually begins, know which of the visionary's ideas to incorporate and which to leave unused because you cannot use them all. Once the project has begun, the visionary's liability is "scope creep": always ready with ideas—they say, "Oh, let's add this" or, "let's tweak that" —they can come up with so many ideas and expand your project in so many ways, it will never get done.

One other thought about intelligent visionaries. Attempts to motivate by recognizing and appreciating their efforts is substantially more effective than praising their intellectual gifts. This seems particularly applicable following a series of failures. Those acknowledged for effort seem measurably more resilient and continuously engaged than those whose intellect is over stressed.

THE START-TO-FINISH THINKER

A talented and gritty mountain climber and professional speaker, Todd Skinner, taught his listeners about "getting on the wall." His experience in free climbing many of the most challenging vertical ascents in the world taught him that the time eventually arrives when planning must be declared adequate and climbing started. And, more importantly, by "getting on the wall," you learn what you never could have learned any other way—you *become* capable.

Start-to-finish thinkers on projects are get-on-the-wall types. They are anxious to get going and start doing. They think about what they need to do first and then they get started. They believe you are not fully capable when you start, but become capable as you progress, so the sooner you start, the better.

This approach is based on the belief you can't know all that will happen or plan for every contingency. If you wait until you get all the answers, you'll just never start. The start-to-finish thinker is anxious to get going, to get on the wall. Building the initial One-Page Project Manager (OPPM) starts at the beginning. They reason: "We need to start with this, and then move on to that . . . and then that . . ." until complete. You may soon find them losing a little focus as the planning becomes increasingly granular or prolonged.

In IT projects, you will discover a concentration of start-to-finish thinkers working primarily in programming and not so many gravitating to the business analysis roles.

As a general rule, they are not particularly outstanding delegators. They have learned that they do things well. They are confident. They are highly effective individual contributors. Handing off work to others is difficult. They may even feel some level of guilt when delegating to others what they themselves could do.

Start-to-finish thinkers are essential to a team because of the energy they bring and their focus on the task. You want them because of all the things they're focused on. They work to meet deadlines. The visionary concentrates on a project's scope, often venturing beyond; the start-to-finish player thinks about how to complete the task on time.

THE FINISH-TO-START THINKER

You will find finish-to-start thinkers in the libraries of any major college. They have their pencils lined up, their calendars telling them when they plan to study for every class, and their books in order.

On a project team, they picture in their mind every project in its finished form. They know what a project will look like when it is done. With the OPPM, they start with the end in mind and build tasks and time lines backward to the beginning.

These are your best planners. They construct the OPPM right to left rather than left to right. Once all the tasks have been identified, they think about filling in the circles. This is in contrast to the visionary thinker who doesn't think about circles or dots at all. The start-to-finish thinker starts filling in circles left to right: this is done first, this is done second, this is done third, and so on. The finish-to-start thinker fills in the plan right to left: if this is the finished product, then to complete it they have to have completed this, and before that they have to complete that. They go backward. They calculate the time to complete a project from the end to the beginning, and as a result, they often end up with a longer time line than, the start-to-finish thinker.

The weakness of finish-to-start thinkers is that they can overplan. The proverbial analysis paralyzes. They do not get on the wall soon enough; they wait and wait to get started. The start-to-finish thinker says, "Give me a couple of ducks," and he's off. The finish-to-start thinker wants all his ducks in a row.

My wife Meredith is a start-to-finish thinker, and I am a finish-to-start thinker. As such, we nicely complement (or clash with) one another. We had a home remodeling project. I did the planning and worried about which were the load-bearing walls and what needed to be done, and I planned and planned. But the weakness of thinkers like me eventually came through, and nothing was getting done. I was undergoing paralysis by analysis. One day I returned home to find Meredith had taken a sledgehammer to a wall and reduced it to rubble. She had enough of my planning and figured it was time to start doing. She did more than "get on the wall," she took down the wall.

A team of all finish-to-start thinkers will overplan your project, and be assured, they will not overspend the budget. Time line—well, that's another story.

Many IT people have found success in this type of thinking. They have learned to "start with the end in mind." For IT projects, however, the "end" is difficult and costly to fully specify because users can't completely identify everything they will need. Therefore, experienced CIO's often partition larger projects into more definable chunks. By bounding both the scope and the time line into more manageable chunks, a propensity for finishing to start thinking is constrained to limiting the planning time. This also provides for some early deliverables while ignoring for the time being, scope that may expand in a future chunk.

Another proven method for addressing these challenges is the "path-based" approach explored by

Harvard Professor David Upton (see "Radically Simple IT," *Harvard Business Review*, March 2008 by David M. Upton and Bradley R. Staats).

I have generally found that finish-to-start thinkers have, as a strength, a natural inclination to delegate and are comfortable surrounding themselves with people who are more competent than they are. They think about what processes or systems are needed for a project and who the best people are to accomplish what is needed, and they can be fearless at going out and getting them.

ASSETS OF THESE THINKERS

- The visionary thinker will assure *innovation* and creativity.
- The start-to-finish thinker gets you moving, brings a "can do" attitude, and is passionate for the *time line*.
- The finish-to-start thinker will be sure the project is well planned and stays on *budget*.

LIABILITIES OF THESE THINKERS

- The visionary guarantees *scope creep* to a project, which affects both cost and the time line. However, scope creep is not always bad.
- The start-to-finish thinker may paint you into a corner by starting things before they are fully thought out, requiring additional money and resources either not planned for or required to *reverse and repair*.

- The finish-to-start thinker is slow to begin and may allow the *time line to slip,* especially in the early planning phase. This is a greater risk for longer projects.

PEOPLE ARE MULTIDIMENSIONAL

People are not one-dimensional. They are multidimensional and possess varying degrees of each type of thinking in their approach to projects. Generally, one type tends to dominate, however.

There are a few remarkable project leaders who are in the triangle in the middle of Figure 3.1. They fire on all pistons, are bright and intuitive, have all sorts of ideas, and jump into a project right away with just the right amount of planning. These are unusual animals.

People who have strengths as visionary and start-to-finish thinkers will get a lot of things started but suffer some false starts. They have a pile of books on their nightstand, all partially read. They are good at starting things, but often lose interest before the project is completed. They are bored easily and crave the thrill of starting something new.

Visionary and finish-to-start thinkers can really slow down a project. They plan things to death and are usually quite risk averse. They visualize how they want to finish a project and then envision a new more expansive conclusion. They have good intensions, but can't get off the starting block. If they are writing a letter, they wait until they get more stationery or have cool postage stamps, and then they'll write and rewrite and rewrite some more. At the end of day, their backwards planning is overcome by evolving vision.

Those who combine finish-to-start and start-to-finish thinking are rare. Give them a set of plans, and they're off doing and accomplishing. On a vacation, they have everything planned. They know what they are going to do each day. They may miss, however, some unique opportunities or unusual activities only contemplated by the creative, visionary thinker.

WHAT THE PROJECT LEADER NEEDS TO DO

The project leader needs all types of thinkers on the project team. This way, the leader can tap the strengths of all of them. The leader also must understand which people are one-dimensional or two-dimensional (the three-dimensional person is so rare you'll have no trouble knowing who they are). In simplest of terms, you need the visionary for the project's scope, the start-to-finish thinker for your time line, and the finish-to-start thinker for your budget.

How to identify who is who: If you think about the people in your organization in terms of these three types of thinkers, you'll probably be able to quickly identify who fits into each category. Start-to-finish are all about getting things going. Finish-to-start thinkers are all about careful planning. Visionary thinkers are all about possibilities.

Pure finish-to-start thinkers are good collaborators. Pure start-to-finish thinkers are quickly engaged. Pure visionaries are not good team members because no one can think as fast as they can. They don't work well on committees; instead, they work within their own minds. Nonetheless, you need all three types on your team.

How do you identify who is who in your company? Walk around your office at 5:00 in the afternoon. The visionaries are alone. They are probably sitting in a chair reading a technical journal or just thinking. Or perhaps they are huddled over their computer keyboard and writing. This is their private time. They are pondering.

The start-to-finish thinkers are busily working. There is paper all over the place; they are fully engaged. The finish-to-start thinkers have an office filled with people. They are writing on white boards, discussing things, and working things out. They are working with their collaborators, planning things, and thinking things through.

No one is good at everything. You need a team with visionary thinkers, start-to-finish thinkers, finish-to-start thinkers, and those who are multidimensional. A team with all of these attributes has great strength, and it can deal with all types of weakness. This is a team that can make the most of the OPPM and be most successful at completing your project.

The One-Page Project Manager for the Project Office

Every project is run from someplace. It could be a small project run from someone's desk and is just one of several responsibilities of that person. Or, it could be a project coordinated from a central office devoted exclusively to corporate project communication. Or it could be a very large project that has its own office.

I suspect most readers of this book work in or with an office with the exclusive responsibility of guiding IT projects. But however the management of projects is set up in your organization, it can be called the Project Office, which I define as the person or group of people who have at least eight high-level, companywide project responsibilities, all focused on seeing that projects are setup and managed for success.

This chapter is about how the Project Office can use the One-Page Project Manager (OPPM) effectively, to address each of these eight project responsibilities.

1. A PROJECT DASHBOARD

The first responsibility of the Project Office is to maintain the dashboard for the organization's projects. By this I mean the Project Office tracks, at a high level, the progress of projects and reports them to upper management. This is a vital responsibility of the Project Office. It reports to the company's executives in a way that allows them to know what is going on with projects and know when attention is needed. The Project Office keeps senior management fully aware, at a high level, of these basic areas:

- The owners, who are those responsible for various parts of a project
- The cost, how much the project has and will cost, and whether it is currently on budget or off budget—and by how much
- The tasks, how the deliverables and activities of the project are progressing versus the plan
- The time line, when various project tasks are finished or are expected to be completed
- The objectives, the what (what the project is) and the why (why it is being done)

The Project Office communicates these aspects of projects to executives for as long as the projects are under development or being completed. The role of the OPPM in the Project Office is to be a tool that efficiently communicates essential information from the Project Office to senior management. I don't think it is an overstatement to say the OPPM is *essential* to an effective Project Office. It is essential because it consolidates all important information in one place. It is a critical communication link between a company's projects and its senior leaders. Think of it as the means by which information flows into and out of a Project Office. And it manages that information by putting it into a form that's easily created, read, and understood. Without the OPPM, the Project Office will be inundated with too much information. With OPPM, their reporting output will be crisp and consolidated into a single page. It is the *dashboard*.

The OPPM makes possible the Project Office's ability to collect, analyze, and report a massive amount of project information. It facilitates the operational efficiency and the communication effectiveness of the Project Office. By requiring every manager to report to you with the OPPM, you only get one page from each. It's a winnowing and summarization tool, as well as the underpinning standard of excellence for a Project Office.

2. A CORPORATE PROJECT METHODOLOGY

The second important responsibility of the Project Office is to be the keeper-of-the-flame, the czar of the company's corporate project methodology. It must also provide tools to support that methodology. Further, the Project Office is responsible for project management systems. The value of the OPPM is, in effect, the communication system. The Project Office uses the OPPM as the methodology for reporting and communicating about projects. As head of a Project Office, I have to make sure every project manager knows how to use the OPPM. Without going too far in making claims for the tool, the OPPM helps promote professionalism in project management within an organization. It provides a protocol from which the discipline of project management can be reinforced.

3. PROJECT TRAINING

Third, the Project Office has the responsibility to train and mentor project managers as they develop their skills. For example, our goal at O.C. Tanner is to have at least 95 percent of our people trained on and using the OPPM at any given time. Our process for doing this: our project managers and those who work on projects read *The One Page Project Manager*, receive general training from me, and specific training from project managers who have worked with the tool, and get encouragement from the Project Office to use the tool. And, of course, it helps that they experience the tool firsthand and discuss its use over time. This allows users to become more familiar and comfortable with it.

In addition to training on the OPPM, other reading materials, lectures, and seminars are encouraged to drive an expanding working knowledge of all aspects of project management's "body of knowledge."

4. CONSISTENT APPLICATION

The Project Office assures the consistent application of the methodology. This takes energy because people want to depart from the standard the organization establishes. Users think they have ways to improve the OPPM or that their project is so special it needs its own version of the OPPM. The Project Office needs to manage such tendencies. It's not that the OPPM cannot be improved or should not be modified for specific situations, but such changes must be done at a high level to prevent balkanization of the tool. If left unchecked, such tendencies will lead, in short order, to many different OPPM formats, therefore, losing the power of standardization and consistency.

The Project Office must balance a standard methodology against continuous improvement. There is real value in consistency. It helps reinforce in the minds of users the value of the tool. It keeps project managers and team members focused on what is important. It makes it easier for everyone in the organization to learn how to create, use, and interpret the tool. Just the right balance between consistency and creativity yields efficiency and excellence.

And it helps management understand what the tool is communicating. Imagine an organization with many projects, each with its fundamentally different OPPM. Senior management will have to decipher what each version of the OPPM is trying to communicate, which negates much of the benefit of having a simple and consistent tool used across an organization, with relatively minor variations for different types of projects. The bottom line: the OPPM is the Project Office's single most important communication tool.

Keep in mind the OPPM does not eliminate, replace, or substitute for any tool your project managers want to use, such as Microsoft Project or a simple time line. It is an addition to the tools you are already using. A major project will have an OPPM at the top and then, drilling down, additional OPPMs for various aspects of the project. With a software project, we might use one OPPM for the hiring of a consultant, another for choosing the software, another for the limited rollout and testing of the software, and so on. At the top is an OPPM that reports on all those under it. It is this top-most OPPM that senior management sees.

The head of projects needs to strike a balance between standardization and customization. What this executive must be on guard for is the tendency of the user to customize the OPPM to the point where it is dramatically different from one project to another, or from one department to another. Certain things *must* remain the same, such as the colors used (and their meanings) and the use of empty circles to convey an aspect of a project not yet completed, and a filled-in circle that signifies completion. The basic matrix in combination with the alignments of owners, tasks, and objectives are essential. These aspects of the OPPM don't change.

But some aspects of the tool can be changed. For example, some projects may use time periods of one week each, while others use monthly periods. Some

OPPMs may incorporate graphs or charts, while others will not. It's the job of the head of the Project Office to exercise the judgment necessary to maintain standards while also allowing creativity, individual ownership, and innovation.

It's important to understand that the Project Office produces a consolidated OPPM that is a summary of all the projects the office is tracking. The project managers for each project submit their OPPMs to the Project Office, where they are, in turn, summarized onto a consolidated OPPM, which is essentially an OPPM that lists all current and recently completed projects. In this way, senior management can quickly see the status of all the projects happening in the organization. If they want more information about individual projects, they can read the OPPMs for those projects, often precluding inefficient inquiry with the project team.

5. PROJECT PUBLIC RELATIONS

I've talked a lot about how the OPPM communicates *up* an organization to senior management. But it also is able to communicate to those within or outside the organization who might have a tangential interest in the particular project. The Project Office can use the tool to market and communicate aspects of a project *out* to audiences who might have a need to know about the project but are not intimately involved with it. Its simplicity makes it a great tool for such communication. Examples of audiences that are communicated to include: suppliers, other managers within the company, the company's human resources department (which wants to keep track of who is working on which projects), the internal audit department, and the sales department (which wants a quick look at how things are progressing on new products so it knows when new products will become available).

By the way, the OPPM has an additional benefit that might not be immediately obvious, namely that it can shorten management meetings. Because everyone is reading from the same page, both literally and metaphorically, when the Project Office holds meetings, participants can quickly get up to speed about the essential aspects of the project. This is a real time saver. So many management meetings are too long. With the OPPM, you can reference back to the tool because everyone knows and understands it. Attention is keen when issues are germane to a person's area of responsibility. When other issues are persued, interest can dissipate. The OPPM helps make discussions clear, concise, and to the point, which is key to keeping everyone engaged.

6. PROJECT PRIORITIZATION

The OPPM helps the Project Office prioritize its portfolio of projects. When the Project Office compiles an OPPM that includes all projects, those that make it onto the tool automatically get priority. They get funded. They get resources ahead of other projects.

It also makes clear the demands that various projects are making on an organization. When a project appears on the corporate OPPM and the reader sees the project involves 303 people, or however many, it reminds everyone of the burden of certain projects and the load these projects are placing on various departments and the organization as a whole. The tool allows management to see the money and people being devoted to various projects and the need to balance the use of those and other resources with the day-to-day activities of the business. It's often difficult to keep projects and daily demands of running a business in proper perspective. Projects are undertaken to make tomorrow's customer orders better, but this may come at the expense of today's orders. The OPPM, because it paints such a clear, readily accessible picture of projects, helps management keep a balance between now and the future.

7. PROJECT REVIEW AND CORRECTIVE ACTION

The consolidated OPPM facilitates the Project Office's and senior management's attention to needed corrective action. The Project Office conducts project reviews prior to reporting on those projects. The OPPM causes the Project Office and the project team to think about the important aspects of a project. Sure, teams will think about time lines and budgets, whether or not they use the OPPM. But they don't often think about who the owners are for each part of a project. Or how various parts of a project relate to important objectives or strategic goals. The OPPM makes these important connections readily apparent.

By using the OPPM, you and your team will have to think about all the essential elements of a project, as well as relationships between parts of the project, plus the people involved with it. And because the OPPM saves time, you will have the time to do this type of thorough planning. The work of the Project Office ends up being more complete and effective because of the OPPM. This might sound more like sales talk than reality, but based on the dozens of projects I've managed with the OPPM and dozens I managed before developing the tool, I can honestly say these benefits are real and valuable.

One more thing: Because the OPPM ties performance to individuals (the owners), when things go well, senior management can see it on the OPPM and take action, such as giving a compliment or otherwise providing positive recognition. The tool helps energize a whole culture of recognition, not just corrective action.

8. PROJECT ARCHIVES AND CONTINUOUS IMPROVEMENT

By holding onto the OPPMs for each project (which is easy to do because even a large project probably has an OPPM generated once a week, which is 52 pages for a one-year project), the Project Office can easily create and maintain an archive of completed projects.

These OPPMs become a repository of project learning. As George Santayana famously said: "Those who cannot learn from history are doomed to repeat it."

Such an archive is a means by which future project leaders and teams can learn. It shows how things were done, how projects progressed, where challenges occurred, and how they were overcome. Using the OPPM to create a history is easy and efficient. And when a project is completed, the Project Office just needs to have all the OPPMs bound and placed in a file cabinet, with electronic copies easily stored and retrieved.

AN EXAMPLE

The PMO provides a monthly report to management which contains the current OPPM for each strategic project. A summary OPPM showing the progress of all the projects serves as the cover page. This summary OPPM for the Project Office must communicate for each corporate project:

- Alignment with company strategy
- Correlation to the annual operating plan
- Capital budget tracking
- Expense budget tracking
- People involved
- Current performance or status
- On time versus lateness
- Assigned project manager
- Executive team responsibilities
- A consolidation and summation

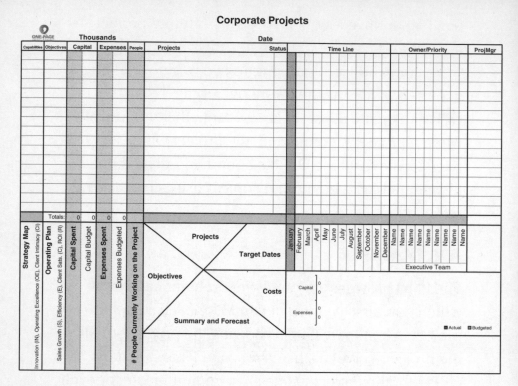

FIGURE 4.1   *Project Office Template.*

This is the heart of the communication network.

Figure 4.1 is a general template. Figure 4.2 is an example from the fictitious Mount Olympus Company. Let's jump right into reading the November year-to-date cover report.

If you look at the fourth heading from the left, you will see Expenses. And at the bottom of the two columns under Expenses are the labels Expenses Spent and Expenses Budgeted. The first reports what has actually been spent, while the second reports on the amount budgeted or what was expected to be spent. The fifth line down, for example, relates to the Zeta Project. It is

Mount Olympus Company
Corporate Projects for 2006
November 2006

ONE-PAGE

Capabilities	Objectives	Capital		Expenses		People	#	Corporate Projects	Status	Time line	Owners/Priority	PM
OE	R	-	-	-	-	12	1	Alpha			B B A B B B B B B	CAC
OE	E	-	-	0	150	30	2	Beta			C B A	DFH
IN	S	-	-	1483	1525	17	3	Gamma			C B A	DFH
IN, OE	S, R	3	3	166	310	16	4	Epsilon			B B B A B	JMV
OE	S	285	450	220	350	11	5	Zeta			B A B B B	JMV
OE	E, D	-	-	-	-	8	6	Eta			A B	STT
CC	S	166	0	132	-	56	7	Theta			A B	TBB
CC	S, D	-	-	-	-	1	8	Iota			A B	TBB
OE	R	-	-	-	-	18	9	Kappa			A C B C C C C C C	SS
CC	S	-	-	-	-	12	10	Lambda			C B B C B B A	HH
OE	E, D	-	-	-	-	13	11	Mu			C B C A C	LTK
OE, CC	S, E, D	-	-	-	-	38	12	Nu			B B B B	SJ
								Completed Projects				
OE	S, R	350	500	65	75	85	1	Xi			B A B	KIG
CC	S	0	0			8	2	Omicron			A B	RSM
OE, CC	S, R	0	0	0	0	300	3	Pi			C B A C B B B B	BLT
OE	S, R	275	217	-	10.2	15	4	Rho			B A B B	CAC
	Totals	1078	1169	2066	2420	640						

Strategy Map
Innovation (IN), Operating Excellence (OE), Client Care (CC)
Sales Growth (S), Efficiency (E), Delivery (D), ROA (R)

Operating Plan
Actual Capital
Capital Budget
Actual Expenses
Expenses Budgeted
People Currently Working on the Project

Projects — Objectives — Target Dates — Costs
Summary and Forecast

January February March April May June July August September October November December

BA TB CC KJ SK JM VN HS DS TT
Executive Team

Capital 1,078 / 1,169
Expenses 2,066 / 2,420
☐ Budgeted ■ Actual

■ = R
■ = G
■ = Y

Iota and Kappa continue to suffer from insufficient IT resources. Zeta remains stalled due to testing failures and scope expansion. New IT people have been hired and are now training to engage on both Iota and Kappa. Zeta remains deadlocked and seriously delayed.

FIGURE 4.2 *Mount Olympus Company Project Office Report.*

budgeted at $350,000 but only $220,000 has been spent, so it is $130,000 under budget. Note, however, that the project is behind schedule.

In fact, if you look under Time Line column, you will see the heavy vertical line, which tells you the month of this OPPM, namely November. Yet, this particular project has four empty dots to the left of this line, indicating the project is four months behind schedule. In fact, three projects are behind schedule, which is indicated by the number of projects whose dots are not filled in all the way to the current time. Eight of the projects are ahead of schedule (which would be indicated by filled-in dots to the right of the heavy vertical line).

A project such as the Epsilon, the fourth project from the top, does not have any dots until May, which is when the project started. The sixth project down, Eta, has dots that stop in October, indicating when the project was projected to end. With these time line dots, you can tell when projects begin and end (or start and continue beyond the scope of this OPPM) and which projects are on time, behind, or ahead of schedule.

The first column on the left is labeled Capabilities. At the bottom of that column are listed the three strategic goals of the company: innovation, operating excellence, and client care. Mount Olympus is committed to be an innovator (IN) in its market, excellent in how it conducts its operations (OE), and superior in how it takes care of its clients (CC). If a project does not address a strategic goal, it should not be done. You can see how each project connects to strategic goals in this column. The Zeta Project has OE in this column, which lets the reader know that this project is tied into the company's strategic goal of being an excellent operating organization.

The second column to the right addresses operating goals. These include sales growth (S), efficiency (E), delivery (D), and return on assets (R), and are short-term rather than strategic. These are self-evident except perhaps for delivery, which has references to on-time delivery of products as a critical requirement of client satisfaction. The operating purpose of the Zeta Project is to spur sales, so this project is tied to the operating goal of sales growth.

To the left of Expenses is Capital, which refers to a project's capital expenses. Capital expenses typically relate to the purchase of tangible assets such as equipment that have useful lives of more than one year. This is what shows up on the balance sheet, while expenses show up on the income statement. With the Zeta Project, the capital budget is $450,000, of which $285,000 has been invested.

The column to the right of this, labeled People, lists the number of employees involved with the project. This lets management know the number of people committed to any given project at any given time. The Zeta Project involves 11 people (this is both full- and part-time employees, and not full-time equivalents or FTEs). We're just counting noses, people who are spending some of their time on the project. Experience has shown that attempting to be more granular with the people number is ineffective. Actual hours spent is important, but not critical at this level.

The last column on the right, PM, refers to project manager. The PM for the Zeta Project we've been looking at is John, who is responsible for this project. Just to the left of this is a heading reading Owners and Priorities. These are the senior managers under whose department the project is being carried out. Folks running the projects and having ownership of them are listed by their priority of importance (A owners own the project with principal responsibility, while B and C owners are helpers with decreasing responsibility).

The status column in the middle of the page (which will print in color) indicates the general performance of each project. If green, the project is going well—its time line and budget are basically where they should be. There is no cause for concern. Yellow indicates there are some issues, but there is still time to recover; these are not projects senior management needs to be worried with at the present time. The project may be a bit behind schedule, a bit over budget, or have some other concern, but in the end, the project should be completed in an acceptable fashion without much intervention from senior management. The red rectangles are projects in trouble. The status of both the Zeta and Iota projects are shown red. The Zeta Project, as noted, is four months behind schedule. Such projects often require intervention from senior management who can secure cross-department assistance or reset priorities.

The rectangle near the lower right-hand corner of the consolidated OPPM shows the consolidated capital and expense budgets. The Capital budget totals $1,169,000, of which $1,078,000 has been spent. The Expense budget totals $2,420,000, of which $2,066,000 has been spent. These are green, indicating there is, overall, no cause for concern relating to the budgets.

The four projects listed below the heavy horizontal line near the middle of the page—Xi, Omicron, Pi, and Rho—are recent projects that have been completed. You can tell they are finished because all circles are filled in, and they have no open circles in the time line.

In the rectangle at the bottom of the page is the Summary and Forecast. It mentions that projects Iota and Kappa continue to suffer from insufficient IT resources. Zeta remains stalled due to testing failures and scope expansion. New IT people have been deployed on Iota and Kappa. Zeta remains deadlocked and seriously delayed. You want to succinctly answer the questions posed by delays in the schedules, and the reds and yellows. After your explanations, give a high-level forecast of future expectations.

With this consolidated OPPM from the Project Office, senior management can quickly see how all projects are progressing, how they're linked to strategies, and who owns them. With a quick read of this tool, all of this can be gleaned by the CEO and others. Providing so much detail in easily digestible form helps the Project Office fulfill its objective to communicate the progress of the company's projects. It helps the Project Office achieve the eight prime objectives mentioned at the start of this chapter.

1. A Project Dashboard
2. A Corporate Project Methodology
3. Project Training
4. Consistent Application of the Methodology
5. Project Public Relations
6. Project Prioritization
7. Project Review and Corrective Action
8. Project Archives and Continuous Improvement

As you can now see, the OPPM is essential to an effective Project Office.

Recognition@work: Launching a New Internet Business

By the late 1990s, every company of significant size in the United States was considering how the Internet would affect their business. So many wondered how to partake of the online gravy train or worried that the gravy train would roll over them and leave them in the virtual dust.

O.C. Tanner was a little different. A get-rich IPO and dotcom exit strategy was not an option. Rather, utilizing this emerging technology to better serve our clients was essential. Beginning in late 1999 and all through the following year, we studied our business seeking to leverage the potential presented by the Internet. In January 2001, while still in the midst of changing our IT infrastructure (as discussed in the next chapter), we launched a dot-com only business. Initially called Entrada, it is today known as recognition@work. It is a performance recognition business which has expanded steadily and revenues grew more than 30 percent in 2008.

THE RECOGNITION@WORK BUSINESS

Briefly, here's how the business works. People at a participating company can, using the Web, nominate a colleague to be recognized for notable performance. An online wizard helps the nominator determine the level of award that is appropriate for the performance being recognized. A manager at the company, who is authorized to do so, approves the award. Once approved, the nominator learns of the approval via the Internet. The nominator then, via the Internet, prints out a certificate that cites the high-performing employee. He then conducts a small ceremony at the company's facilities where the employee is recognized in front of his or her peers.

The recipient receives the certificate which contains an access code. He goes online and, using the code, gets access to the recognition@work range of awards that have been approved for his or her level of achievement. The recipient chooses the desired recognition award, which is then shipped to his home or office. This business provides, via the Internet, an efficient and effective way for companies to appreciate employees who have performed with distinction. Research on the power of recognition to engage employees coupled with a positive correlation with greater financial performance is reported and explained in *The Carrot Principle* by Chester Elton and Adrian Gostick (New York: Free Press, 2007).

Companies are reaching out to assess their recognition effectiveness and determine its impact on manager relevance and employee engagement. OC Tanner's suite of solutions includes best practice research, books, publications, speaking, training, and awards celebrating service milestones and performance.

Tanner's value resides in customer intimate solutions that enable clients to achieve their objectives by powering appreciation to communicate what matters most to them. When recognition becomes embedded in a company's culture, measurable results begin to emerge.

Our assignment was to create a new offering. Because this project involved building an internet-based performance recognition business from scratch, the One-Page Project Manager (OPPM) I used is more complicated than the typical one. Quite honestly, this is not an OPPM for the novice. If you've never created and used an OPPM, don't make this your first. It is better that you use a simpler OPPM for one or two projects before wading into the waters of using this tool for creating a new IT business. Alternatively, given that this book is written for IT professionals and given that the OPPM is substantially easier to use than other tools you are accustomed to—go for it!

The One-Page Project Manager—On Steroids

The standard OPPM takes up the bottom half of the form. This is the template we have discussed throughout this book (and also in my first book, *The One-Page Project Manager,* Hoboken, NJ: Wiley, 2006). We discuss some unique variations applicable to IT projects at the end of this chapter.

However, the upper half of the tool is unique to this project (Figure 5.1).You can see at the bottom left-hand

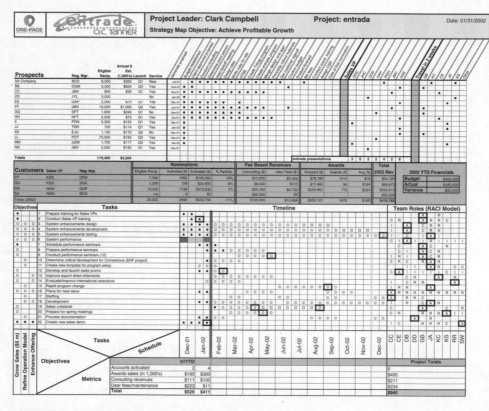

FIGURE 5.1   *The January Recognition@work Report.*

corner that the subobjectives are to grow sales
(the initial goal was $5 million), refine our operation
(which meant having the operation and the underlying
system work well), and enhance our offering (which
meant adding system functionality, together with giving
recipients more award choices).

This form really addresses two issues: the launching
and the running of a business.

I recommend you go to www.onepageprojectmanager.
com, download this form, and print it using a color
printer. You will find it easier to match the following
explanations if you don't have to keep referring back to
Figure 5.1, and the form will be larger and in color.

Near the bottom right of the form, you will see a
group of columns each with the initials of the 10 people
who made up our project team.

Rather than the real names, the initials are shown
throughout these examples in order to protect
confidentiality. Complete names of people and
companies were clearly shown in the forms actually used.

The top half of the form has two main sections:
Prospects and Customers. The activities in the top half
of the OPPM were designed to take a prospect and
migrate them into an ordering customer, and then take
current customers and follow nominations, awards
selected, and various components of services revenue.

Under Prospects in the upper left-hand corner of the
tool, we list the Prospect, the O.C. Tanner Regional
Manager who is handling the account, Eligible
Recipients (the number of employees at the prospect
who would be eligible to participate in this awards

recognition program—this represents the size of our market at this particular prospect), Annual $ Est. (the estimated dollar amount of business the prospect may offer to O.C. Tanner), Launch (the quarter we expect to launch them as a new customer of recognition@ work), and Service (whether they are currently a service award client). Note that at the bottom of Eligible Recip. and Annual $ Est. are totals. The first, under Eligible Recip., is the total number of eligible employees (our total market, in effect) if all of these prospects become customers. The other total, under Annual $ Est., is the total amount of potential business we could win if all of these prospects become customers.

In the section directly to the right of the one we just discussed, the first column is titled, Generate proposal. This refers to the date the proposal was given to the prospect. The remaining columns are pretty much self-explanatory, with a few exceptions. The column labeled HTML refers to whether we have written HTML software code for the client. Create Trilogy program is whether we have programmed the client into the Trilogy software program, which handles orders and pricing. The column labeled Assign CSR, refers to whether we have assigned a client service representative to the prospect.

The next section to the right, Sales Vice Presidents, identifies which of our sales vice presidents (they work in different geographic areas of the country) has been assigned to this prospect. The final section to the right, Travel in 2 weeks, identifies which team member will be traveling to the prospect within the next in two weeks.

The sections below the ones just discussed are shaded and labeled Customers. These are companies that were once prospects but have become current customers. The initials to the left identifies the customer and the sales vice president and Regional Manager responsible for that customer. As we discussed before, with the OPPM, we attach a name to the various tasks, which is a constant reminder and motivator. One of the powerful qualities of the OPPM is how clearly it spells out and aligns ownership—who owns and is responsible for what.

Let's first follow the development of a prospective client. Consider prospect EE going from left to right we see that the Regional Manager is DAP. There are 2000 eligible award recipients and potential award revenue of $75,000. They plan a first quarter launch and are a current service award customer. Continuing to the right, the proposal was generated on December 1. The seven dark circles correspond with the 18 tasks necessary to complete prior to becoming a customer and placing their first nomination. On the right, you note that KSS is the sales vice president in whose region this prospect resides and that JA will be traveling to visit with this prospect in the next two weeks.

Running along the bottom of the prospect section, you see that the pipeline of potential clients sums to 119,400 eligible recipients and $3.2 million in revenue.

The Entrada presentations line gives some indication of how aggressively each sales vice president is pushing this new business. KSS, with 6 presentations in his area, is significantly more successful than JHC at 0. Also you see with a glance at the top right where each of your team is traveling in the next two weeks.

Let's look at customer PP and follow its analysis across the OPPM. It is managed by Sales vice president KSS, and handled by Regional Manager DFM. This client has 7,500 employees eligible to receive a recognition award as seen in the column titled Eligible Recip. The next column, Activated (#), tells us the number of nominations (1,350) given or activated, which refers to the number of employees who have been nominated and approved for an award. The following column, Activated ($) shows how much revenue these awards total ($105,300) if they are all chosen and ordered. We include this number because, while these employees have been approved for awards, they haven't yet ordered their awards. For us, therefore, this is expected future revenue. The next column, Percent Participation, is the percentage of the total employees eligible who have been granted awards.

The following section, Fee Based Revenues, lists the consulting fees and user fees collected from this client so far— $10,000 in consulting and $5,400 in fees.

The Awards section provides information on the dollar amount of awards that have actually been ordered and shipped ($78,780), the number of awards shipped (1,010), and the average value of the awards (the first column divided by the second, which in the case of customer PP is $78). The next column, Total 2002 Rev, totals up all the revenue we received from this client in 2002. The total revenue we've received in 2002 from customer PP is $94,180. At the bottom of this column is

the sum of revenue, $410,765 we have received from
all the new business.

The final section, 2002 YTD Financials, sums up the
financials year-to-date, including the total cost of the
project itself, which we here call Budget ($400,000).
Next is how much we have actually spent of this budget,
called Actual ($430,000), and the difference between
what's been budgeted and what's been spent, Variance,
which is $30,000 over budget.

Information we needed about the progress of the
launch, such as conversion of prospects to customers,
potential market, revenues generated and more, are
spelled out in the top portion of the tool. This is much
like a customer dashboard.

The bottom section is the customary OPPM template
refined a little for IT projects.

You will note the usual objectives section has been
condensed down into three subobjectives, and then
aligned with each task. The schedule is for 13 months
beginning with December 2001 and extending through
December 2002. The reporting "buckets" are twice per
month.

As in the standard template, each task is aligned with
subobjectives, time line plan, time line performance,
and owners.

Task #1, Prepare training for sales VPs, is shown
complete. Task #3, System enhancement design, is on
schedule; however, you will see four open boxes added
to the end of the time line. This shows an extension to
the time line beyond the original plan. Task #4 has also
been extended. By focusing on the new open squares,

your refined time line expectations are communicated. These tasks have been extended, with Task #19, Sales collateral, stretched out eight periods or four months. A bold outline around the time box indicates a major milestone. It is easy to spot the nine major milestones for this project. Each major milestone clearly shows its task, its owner, its completion date, and most important progress toward completion.

The major milestones for task #2 and #22 have been accomplished. One is coming due quickly with task #12, with others dotting the landscape of the project.

Experienced IT project managers will quickly see that the combinations of task extension for both design (task #3) and development (task #4) coupled with the approaching major milestones for completing testing raises quality concerns and some worries about the scheduled go-live for enhancements planned for year-end.

A note on the Stage-gate® process and the OPPM: Using an OPPM for each stage (between each gate) is a powerful communication amplification of the product innovation process. The Stage-gate® product innovations and launch process, pioneered and developed by Dr. Robert G. Cooper (see www.stage-gate.com) was an important methodology underpinning the success of launching our Entrada business.

DuPont Chemical Company, my former employer, was an early adopter and successful user of Stage-gate®. Most IT people reading this book are familiar, and possibly trained, on this project management road map for driving innovation from initial ideas to final product launch.

Simply said, the Stage-gate® process divides the climbing of this massive and unknown mountain into distinct stages separated by management decision gates. Remembering Todd Skinner's comments about "getting on the wall," the Stage-gate® process wraps a standard methodology around the innovative discovering—the "becoming" which occurs in the "doing."

The OPPMs used for each stage prior to launching the 1.0 version of Entrada are not shown here. Even product enhancements are greatly facilitated by stage-gating, as well as other project management tools like Microsoft Project®. The five gates and five stages accompanied by a full Microsoft project plan are operating in the background while only a few tasks are shown on the OPPM.

As I've said, the OPPM does not replace these powerful and often-necessary project management tools—it complements and communicates.

Another common IT technique fits perfectly into the OPPM format—the RACI model. RACI is a relatively straightforward tool used in communicating roles and responsibilities of each project stake holder or team member.

As a reminder, RACI is an abbreviation for

R = Responsible

A = Accountable

C = Consulted

I = Informed

- *Responsible:* This person is the doer, the one who does the work. There can be more than one R for each task. Start-to-Finish thinking is valuable here.

- *Accountable:* This person is the owner, the one ultimately answerable for the task. There should only be one A for each task. A good project manager will aggressively delegate As and Rs. finish-to-start thinking helps here.

- *Consulted:* This person is an advisor, typically a subject matter expert who should be consulted *prior* to actions or decisions. Visionary thinking is a critical element here.

- *Informed:* This person should be made aware by being informed *after* the actions or decisions.

Referring back to our OPPM for the Entrada project, you see the 10 members of the project team shown in the lower right-hand corner of the form and the box above their initials showing their ownership and alignment to each task.

For IT projects, the RACI model replaces the simple A, B, C designations used in the standard template.

The team must do the construction and completion of their part of the OPPM. Thorough understanding and full agreement must be reached prior to presenting your completed OPPM to upper management for approval. Discussion of this section with upper management provides the perfect foundation for refining and clarifying your understanding of their expectations concerning you and your teams, accountability and responsibility coupled with management's desire for prior-consultation and postinformation.

Once your RACI box is complete, both a vertical and horizontal analysis can provide valuable insight and may even suggest source changes and refinements, which could involve every component of your OPPM.

I put a bold outline around the As to clearly communicate the ultimate owner.

Finally, the metrics section for this project is a chart showing financial progress: $529,000 in all of 2001 and $411,000 for the first two months of 2002—totaling $940,000 for the full project revenue-to-date.

Managing an Enterprise Resource Planning Project

Computers and the software that run them have a limited life span. And when business requirements are changing rapidly, driving aggressive development and change in the supporting technology, pressure grows to enable business processes and support clients with the advantages of new technology.

That was what we at O.C. Tanner faced. We had in place aging mainframe computers and the associated software that went with them. By the late 1990s, it had become clear that this technology was inhibiting our success and it was time to move to client-server-based hardware and state-of-the-art software.

SOME BACKGROUND

To understand how the use of the One-Page Project Manager (OPPM) evolved over the life of this project, you need some background. We called the project Cornerstone, since IT supported business processes are a cornerstone of our business, and this project involved deciding what to buy to replace our legacy systems and then installing it. For a year prior to launching the project, we evaluated various hardware platforms and software packages. We hired top-notch (and pricey) consultants to help us.

At the end, we decided to move to a three-tier client-server environment, replacing our DOS-based environment with a graphical user interface. As IT people know, the three tiers are the client tier, the application tier, and the database tier. Specifically, we chose: a hardware platform from Hewlett-Packard (HP) which included servers, PCs, and the like; a front-end package that does sales, orders, and pricing functions from Trilogy; and an enterprise resource planning (ERP) package from SAP that provided back office and financial functions.

We started planning for this project in early 1998 with our consultants, the Gartner Group, and launched the implementation project in January 1999. The goal was to complete the project by the end of 1999, in time to deal with Y2K. Helping us implement the project was the consulting arm of Arthur Andersen. The budget for the entire Cornerstone project: $30 million.

An important point to remember: The OPPM sits on top of all other tools used by the project manager.

It does not supplant others and must be correlated with and aligned to the other tools used in projects. An OPPM was used initially in 1998 to manage Gartner's efforts to select the vendors. What was supposed to then be a one-year deployment turned into a multiyear multiproject. For the multiyear implementation project, we decided to create a different OPPM for each year as the project proceeded. In the beginning of 1999, for example, we used an OPPM involved with the design and deployment of the back office, front office, and financial software packages on HP hardware. Since we knew very little about the newly acquired technology, the OPPM principally covered a consolidation of methodologies and project plans supplied by the various vendors.

There were different OPPMs for 2000, 2001, and 2002 as well, each reflecting a little more learning on the part of our project team, and therefore both a refinement of and a growing departure from "vanilla" methodologies. The example we use in this book is the OPPM for 2002, the final year of the Cornerstone project (Figure 6.1).

Let me stop and confess right here that our Cornerstone project is a story of how we recovered, along the way, after some very serious mistakes. It is a saga of how we learned from our stumbles and struggled to turn them into the proverbial stepping-stones.

During the early stages of the project, we invited Todd Skinner, rock climber and author, to speak to us. Todd Skinner is credited as the "most accomplished

Project Leader: Clark Campbell		Project: Finishing Cornerstone		Date: 05/11/02
Strategy Map Objective: Achieve Profitable Growth				

FIGURE 6.1   *The May Cornerstone Report.*

rock climber of this generation." Of his 300 first ascents in 26 countries, it was his spectacular 60-day free ascent of the east face of 20,500-foot Trango Tower in the Himalayas that inspired us. We were in awe of his determination and stamina, and we were personally tutored by what he learned "on the wall":

- "The mountain is the catalyst that transforms a group into a team."

- "What you don't know, the mountain will teach you."
- "Each mountain is made up of rope lengths, and each rope length is made up of single steps."
- "It's not if you fall . . . but the knowledge you acquire from the fall and the way you apply it."
- "The severity and duration of a storm are less important than mind-set, momentum, and morale.

Many times while "on the wall" of our Cornerstone project, we referred back to Todd Skinner's insight to help us maintain our tenacity, courage, and focus on the summit.

Now, back to the facts. Actually, this project had its earliest beginnings in 1997, when we began considering how we would reengineer our business. This was a project that would transform our entire enterprise. At this early stage, we laid out three phases for the entire project:

1. An analysis of our current business model, a potential future state, gaps, and a future IT assessment;
2. Request for proposal (RFP) to vendors to implement our assessment; and
3. A high level migration plan to take us from where we were with our legacy system to where we would decide we wanted to be.

By 1998, we were using an OPPM to go through the process and analysis of software and hardware to decide what would be right for us. This was then followed with

RFPs and scrutinizing the responses, including studying proposals and testing demonstration projects. And then we negotiated and signed contracts with vendors. All the while, the OPPM communicated our progress.

On January 2, 1999, our board of directors approved the project. Then the implementation project plan started. The OPPM took the high points of each deployment plan from each vendor—SAP, Trilogy, and HP—integrated them, and then wrapped that around how Arthur Andersen would guide us through the transformation. As of April 1999, the financial portion of the project, which was part of the SAP deliverables, went live (on time) for all financials. This was ahead of Y2K, which was important. At around this time, our CIO resigned and a new one was hired.

By December 1999, we realized that the work would be substantially more difficult than we had thought. The 1999 OPPM was largely a compilation, integration, and alignment of the varying plans of the different vendors; these were not well integrated. They were more a parallel series of separate projects, yet not tightly interwoven. Vendors remained committed to their unique methodologies, unwilling to compromise enough to bind into an interdependent whole.

In 2000, it became clear we would have to launch out on our own. The OPPM was the document we used to help us navigate through these issues.

At this time, we launched Cornerstone Lite. Originally, we were advised to do a Big Bang conversion—turn off the legacy system and then turn on the new client-server system over, say, a single weekend. After our experiences with the project the first year and all we had learned since we started Cornerstone, we decided that to shut-it-off-one-day and start-it-up-the-next was far too risky a strategy. We were also not in a position to execute a series of "little bangs." The remaining modules were dependently connected, and we didn't have a fully functional small division to learn from. That's when we devised Cornerstone Lite. We would continue using our legacy system in parallel with the new system as it was gradually eased in. All new business and all new customers would be built into the new system while our existing business would remain on the legacy system and be converted over time.

Adding to the challenge was the decision, in 2001, to launch a new dot-com business (discussed in the previous chapter). This business would be built on the new platform since we were planning to eventually get rid of the old. This meant that not only would we do a Cornerstone Lite while we carefully converted existing clients to the new system, but also we had to add an entire new business at the very same time.

By deciding to go with Cornerstone Lite, we made the commitment to have two systems operating in tandem as we went through the challenges of converting our existing business over to the new system. In the middle of 2001, we had some vigorous debates over the desirability of doing this. If you are familiar with transformation projects such as Cornerstone, it will come as no surprise that our consultants, and just about anyone else we talked to, said we should never run two systems at once. Nonetheless, we did. And we are thankful we did.

Keep in mind that in 1999, as was reflected in our OPPM, we had a collection of projects that were aligned according to the plans of various vendors, as I mentioned earlier. By 2000 and 2001, we had to slowly disconnect from their plans (which were based on the Big Bang strategy) and connect to our plans. The owners of the project, as shown on the OPPM, went from being consultants to being a combination of O.C. Tanner employees and consultants, to finally being O.C. Tanner employees exclusively. By the end of 2001, all the business and technical leaders came from in-house—and all the consultants moved on. Not only were all the consultants (and at their peak, we had 60 consultants on our premises) no longer business or technical leaders, they were gone. Period. We brought the entire project in-house. We had also exhausted our consulting budget.

The tasks, as specified on the OPPM, went from being delineated by the vendors, to tasks that our own team drew up and committed to completing. By this time, our people had gone through an aggressive learning curve; it was trial by fire. The team knew much more of which we needed to accomplish and how to measure it. The mountain was teaching us what we needed to know.

Let's talk about how expenditures evolved. Early in the project, most costs were for software and consultants, many of whom were brilliant and absolutely indispensable to our success.

They came from SAP, Arthur Andersen, and Trilogy. By the middle of project, most costs were associated with the purchase of HP hardware. And by the latter part of the project, costs were largely those associated with our own people.

The time lines, as reflected in our initial OPPMs, were taken on faith as bestowed on us by the consultants. We worried about these time lines, but trusted the consultants. As we progressed and better understood the software, hardware, and the challenges involved, the time lines became more and more determined by O.C. Tanner and less and less by the consultants.

Notable was how the attitudes and feelings of ownership of people in our company changed. In the beginning of the project, our people would talk about the project by saying, "they said this," or "they did that." The "they" were the consultants. As the project progressed, our people started talking about "we think" and "we know." There was a remarkable infusion of ownership within our company. The mountain was the catalyst.

In addition, the subobjectives changed. At first, meeting the time lines was very important because time lines were tied to costs and the longer we went; the longer we needed the consultants (I won't mention the dollars involved, but trust me, those scores of consultants were not cheap). When the time lines were under pressure, we would do tradeoffs—we would limit scope so we could meet deadlines. We reached a point where we didn't want to do that anymore. We were cutting into muscle. By moving to our internal people who could do what the expensive consultants could do for a lot less, our priorities shifted from meeting deadlines to achieving the scope we needed so our business could run efficiently and competitively. Of course, our people could not immediately do what the consultants could. This forced our people to reach beyond their grasp. We really did not have any choice: We could not afford the full brigade of consultants over a protracted period of time.

We abandoned the recommended go-live methodology—the Big Bang. We decided to operate our two systems in tandem because stability and scope were more important than the time line. The new robust functionality we wanted to offer our clients could only be rapidly achieved through our Cornerstone Lite strategy. Once the project was brought in-house and costs contained, the timing was not pressed by the budget. We were able to add functionality. This became important. In fact, we allowed some scope creep, such as the building of the Internet business right on top of Cornerstone.

Prior to the decision to proceed with Cornerstone Lite, several planned go-lives were announced and then eventually abandoned. We nearly fell off the mountain. However, at that moment, four critical elements came together to open a new path:

1. A patient and encouraging board and senior management that was communicated to honestly each step of the way by OPPMs.
2. A weathered, enabled, and determined team on the wall that was committed to seeking a "future better beyond our present best."

3. A change in methodology—to promise the delivery of just a chunk—Cornerstone Lite for newly acquired accounts only.

4. The absence of the go-live pressure of the expensive consultant run-rates.

Cornerstone Lite came live on time as promised! Chunks of conversion were now planned.

The new level of functionality began to manifest itself as the project progressed. As new customers came onboard, they were placed on the new system. Gradually, old clients were converted to the new system. On-time delivery, the amount of orders entered, the amount of orders shipped, order accuracy, inventory levels—these general business metrics became critical to the project as performance and stability measures.

With the growth of the OPPM structure, we recognized that a greater number of our objectives were subjective rather than objective. For example, initially, we might have asked about a part of the system: Is it now live? This would result in a yes-or-no answer. But a subjective objective would be: When you hit the button, does it work? "Work" is a subjective concept. Subjective colors become more dominant on the OPPM. The OPPMs of the early years were filled primarily with *dots*—objective time lines and milestones. Some of our contracts were fixed-fee, also driving consultants to give higher priority to time line over functionality.

Another major change related to the business. In the first part of the project, we carefully monitored consultant costs, but in the latter part of project, that cost tracking almost went away because the costs were now the costs of our own people. *We went from managing the costs of consultants to managing the system performance and the metrics of our own business.*

USING THE ONE-PAGE PROJECT MANAGER

Where objective tasks are generally at the top of the OPPM, subjective tasks went to the top of the Cornerstone OPPM, reflecting their importance. In the color boxes, there are also the letters Y, G, and R. Because so many people were following the project we didn't want to incur the expense of printing the OPPMs in color for everyone so we used letters (Y = Yellow, G = Green, and R = Red) allowing us to use black and white photocopies to communicate.

In the lower left-hand corner of the OPPM, we divided the final portion of the project into three objectives:

1. Single System and Processes (this refers to us getting all our information technology running on one system);
2. Stable System and Processes (the system and processes would be stable and predictable); and
3. Enhanced System and Processes (the new system would be enhanced, expanded, and more robust than the system it was replacing).

This project had two types of owners, rather than the usual one—a *lead-pair*. Each component needed a ERP Implementation business owner who was someone from the business side of the company—client relations, customer service, manufacturing, accounting. These were the people who use the system. In addition, there was a technical lead, an IT professional, the person who managed the programming and implemented the system. One of the many things we learned while "on the wall," was this concept of a lead-pair. The natural tendency was to allow the technical person to lead by default since they understood the technology. This led to robust programs that were inadequate for the users. Consultants advised us to always have a person from the business side to provide the final say. This led to inefficient programming and technical architectural problems. A few technical leads each connected to the larger group of business leads all indicated clearly on the OPPM facilitated an "equally yoked" commitment and mutual cooperation.

Let's look at the project on line 3 (again, printing a color copy off the web will assist you here): Client Communication: Business Lead DDD is in charge of this task from the business side. Under Technical Lead, there is an A in the second column, indicating Technical Lead BG has A (primary) responsibility for this task. The two leads work together to bring this task home.

Notice that in December 01 on the OPPM, the Time line box is not divided into two as it is in the other months. By dividing each month into two, we are saying we will measure our performance twice each month, but in December, we will measure it only once (because of the holidays).

Take a look at the project on line 5: Finance. Notice it went red in the second half of February and now, in May (at the time of this OPPM) it remains red. This means the Finance project continues to be a problem. Also notice that this project has two A technical leads. We sometimes use multiple leads on technical projects, but we do not use multiple business leads.

Consider Project 21: Account Conversions, which refers to converting clients to the new system. In boldface type is written (40%). This is the amount of incentive bonus tied to this deliverable. The Project 10 line shows another 40 percent aligned with recognition award on-time delivery, while the remaining 20 percent, not seen on the OPPM, is for individual performance. We wanted to motivate our people to convert clients to the new system but not at the expense of client satisfaction. It felt as though we were expanding our capacity just barely ahead of demand. Even though project scope and client care took precedence over the original time line, the necessity of a continued focused attention on timing was required in order to drive accomplishment and preclude scope creep.

Project 21 sits between the subjective and objective tasks because it is both qualitative and quantitative. This is why it has two lines indicating how it is progressing. The black dots indicate we are doing okay on the number of planned conversions. The different colors are in reference to the quality of conversions, such as their stability and accuracy. While the performance here was a bit shaky between November and February where you see red and yellow boxes, from late February on, there is only green, signifying the conversion process is going well. In fact, partly as a result of his performance on this task, amplified by the visibility of the OPPM by senior management, Business Lead STJ was eventually promoted to vice president. This is an example of the OPPM serving as a wonderful way to communicate outstanding performance.

Note that the Proposed Wizard Enhancements on line 2 of the quantitative tasks is seriously behind schedule. Several other quantitative tasks (see lines 4, 6, 10, 13, and 14) have been completed and closed.

The first line under metrics is Mainframe Cost ($1,000s). This refers to the monthly lease payments for the mainframe in thousands of dollars. The nonconverted accounts are resident on the mainframe, and when conversion is complete, this mainframe cost will be terminated.

The second line, # Converted Accounts, tells in the first column the number of accounts converted in total, and the subsequent columns show the number of accounts converted in each month. Line three % Orders on Time, is a reference to the percent of orders delivered on time. On-time delivery was a problem with the legacy system. Now the percentage of on-time deliveries is improving, though there was some backpedaling in April. I am delighted to say that as this writing in 2008, on-time delivery continues at better than 99%, substantially better than prior to Cornerstone.

The next line, $ Shipments ($1,000s) is the amount of shipments in thousands of dollars resident in the new system. The next line refers to the percentage of a year's shipments the previous line represents. In the first column, 01 YTD (year to date), it says that 20 percent of the year's shipments totaled $53,989,000. As shipments are added in each month, this percentage increases 42 percent in January, increasing to 59 percent by April, or 51 percent of all orders, January through April.

In the lower right-hand corner, 02YTD or Total, you find the total for the year to date for 2002. For Mainframe Cost, the total is $880,000. For # Converted Accounts, there have been 8,793 accounts converted out of 10,000 which is the target number for the year. With % Orders on Time, 89 percent of the orders year-to-date have shipped on time. Year-to-date, $40,607,000 worth of orders has been shipped (Jan. 02 through April 02).

How is the project performing? The OPPM shows both the six-month history as well as the current status middle of May.

It is easy to see the history of challenges and victories over time for qualitative projects 1 through 21 noting that in December half were yellow or red, and by the time of this report only 3 yellows and one red.

The quantitative measures are also clearly seen: 4 are ahead of schedule, 5 are complete and closed, 1 is abandoned, and 3 are behind schedule.

To be quite candid, this level of performance was not always the case. The OPPM for the earlier years showed an abundance of red and some substantial lateness across a large group of tasks. Our CEO kept the following posted behind his desk:

In the beginning of any project there is great enthusiasm,

followed by doubt,

then panic,

searching for the guilty party,

and finally punishment of the innocent,

and rewarding the uninvolved.

—Helmut Schmidt, German Chancellor

During some of the darkest days of the Cornerstone Project, this reminded us that we were "on the wall" together even when the wind howled, the snow raged, and our ropes were frozen to the face of the mountains.

Managing Consultants

Until now, I've referred to the One-Page Project Manager (OPPM) solely as a communication tool. It is that, of course. But in fact, it can be used as something more—a tool to communicate *and* a tool to manage. I use the OPPM to manage consultants, whom we have hired for a wide variety of projects, but who are particularly common with IT projects.

Recently, we hired an international consulting firm to help us with a pricing project. We wanted to evaluate our pricing strategy to better align our prices with the value we provide our clients.

The OPPM I created for the project had three uses:

1. It communicated to upper management and other interested parties how the project was progressing, which is the traditional use of the tool;
2. It helped us manage the consultants; and

3. It was used *by the consulting firm to manage us.* Yes, we got some of our own medicine back when the consulting firm turned the tables and used the OPPM to help them keep us going in the proper direction. In fact, all parties benefited from using the OPPM.

The project involved two phases. The OPPM samples found in this chapter show the tool completed for the first phase and as a plan waiting to be implemented for the second phase. I chose these two phases so you could see the OPPM completed and empty.

PHASE 1: ONE-PAGE PROJECT MANAGER

Notice the two OPPMs (Figures 7.1 and 7.2) are fairly standard-issue types, the sort we have seen in other chapters with a few variations. Let's look at Phase 1 first. The header contains the Name of the project, Pricing Strategy (Phase 1); the Project Leader and the Project Objective; Developing a Strategy to Align Prices with Value Provided.

In the matrix portion (in the lower left), you'll notice Target Dates (Week ending). This line shows the OPPM followed the project in one-week intervals and it ran for 12 intervals or 12 weeks. At the very lower left-hand corner were the project's subobjectives: Data Gathering, Data Analysis, and Conclusions and Recommendations. In order to reach our Project Objective, we needed to accomplish these three subobjectives.

The column headed Major Tasks lists 22 quantitative tasks (numbered 1 through 22) plus two qualitative tasks (labeled A and B).

Project Leader: Clark Campbell	Project: Pricing Strategy (Phase 1)	Date: 12/08/06

Project Objective: Developing a Strategy to Align Prices with Value Provided

Objectives	Major Tasks		Project Completed By: December 7, 2006	Owner/Priority
	1	Interview and choose consultants		A A
	2	Secure approval and budget to proceed		A
	3	Provide OCT accounting data		A B
	4	Provide OCT compensation data		A B
	5	Provide OCT customer data		A B
	6	Provide OCT marketing data		A B
	7	Provide OCT pricing data		A B
	8	Provide OCT sales data		A B
	9	Provide OCT survey data		A B
	10	Recommend potential deal reconstruction candidates		A B
	11	Collect and analyze internal transaction and deal data		A B
	12	Exploratory interviews with internal stakeholders		A B A
	13	Review existing research results		A A
	14	"If project ended today..." working document		A A
	15	Apply PSKG Scorecard		A B A
	16	Apply PSKG ComStrat		A B A
	17	Apply PSKG Case Benchmarks		A A
	18	Conduct selected # of deal reconstructions (8–12)		A B A
	19	Assimilate analyses into recommendations		
	20	Deliver recommendations Dec 6–7		A B B A
	21	Phase 2 go ahead (OC Tanner)		
	22	Run pricing simulation exercise (Moved to 2007)		
	A	OC Tanner Performance		
	B	PSKG Performance		

# People working on the project:	12	12	14	14	15	40	40	15	15	15	15	15

Target Dates (Week ending): Sep-22, Sep-29, Oct-06, Oct-13, Oct-20, Oct-27, Nov-03, Nov-10, Nov-17, Nov-24, Dec-01, Dec-08

Owners: FL (PSKG), CC (OCT), BT & Team, PSKG Team

Left axis: Data Gathering, Data Analysis, Conclusions & Recommendations

Major Tasks — Target Dates — Objectives — Costs — Summary and Forecast

Phase 1: Actual $ / Budget $
Expenses: Actual $ / Budget $
☐ Phase 1 ■ Expenses   ■ = G   ☐ = Y

Final recommendations delivered on Dec 6 and Dec 7 in Salt Lake City to the Pricing Study Team and the Operating Leaders.
Overall, Tanner responded positively to the final recommendations.
Next steps: PSKG will forward the final presentation on to the group, integrating comments as needed. Also awaiting approval to begin Phase 2 value-based segmentation study.

FIGURE 7.1   *The Phase One Consulting Report.*

On the right-hand side near the bottom are the Owners. This is different than in other OPPMs we've discussed. I've said before that owners should always be employees of your company, not outsiders such as consultants. As with any good rule, this rule can and should be broken in a project such as the one we're discussing. The first owner is FL. She is, in fact, an employee of the consulting firm, not of O.C. Tanner. The next two owners, CC and BT & Team are O.C. Tanner employees. The "Team" is the group of our employees

Project Leader: Clark Campbell **Project: Value-Based Segmentation (Phase 2)** Date: 02/16/07

ONE-PAGE — **Project Objective: Developing segment-specific offers to meet customer needs**

Objectives			Major Tasks	Project Completed by June 2007	Owner/Priority
	●	1	Approval for Phase 2 from OC Tanner	●	B B A
			Training Modules (Responsibility of TT)		
○	○	2	Plan & execute training: Operating leaders	● ● ○ ○ ○ ○ ○ ○ ○ ○ ○	A B B C B
○	○	3	Plan & execute training: Sales leadership	○ ○ ○ ○ ○ ○ ○ ○ ○ ○	A B B C B
○	○	4	Plan & execute training: Broader sales team	○ ○ ○ ○ ○ ○ ○ ○ ○ ○	A B B C B
			Survey Design (Responsibility of DS/CC)		
●		5	Hypothesis development with internal support	● ● ●	A B B C C
●		6	Selection of instrument type and interview format	● ● ●	A B C C
●		7	Draft questions, including tradeoff screens	● ●	A B
●		8	Finish questionnaire draft	● ●	A B
○	○	9	Obtain client sign off on questions and trade-off screens	○ ○	A B C B
○	○	10	Finalize questionnaire	○ ○	A B B
○	○	11	Interim review after questionnaire finalized (if needed)	○	A B B C C B
			Survey Execution (Responsibility of DS/CC)		
○	○	12	Selection of market research vendor	○ ○	A B B
○		13	Setting of customer quotas	○ ○	A B
○		14	Develop target customer list	○	A B
○		15	Programming of survey	○ ○	A B
○	○	16	Conduct pilot interview(s) to test questionnaire	○	A B
○		17	Customer recruiting/fielding	○ ○ ○ ○	A B
○	○	18	Delivery of final data from market research vendor	○	A B B
			Survey Analysis (Responsibility of DS/CC)		
○		19	Data cleaning	○ ○	A B
○		20	Cluster analysis	○ ○	A B
○	○	21	Segment profiling	○ ○	A B
○	○	22	Value proposition development	○ ○	A B
○	○	23	Client value pricing guidance by segment	○ ○	A B
○	○	24	Feasibility testing with operations / revised value props	○ ○	A B C C C
○	○	25	Value-in-use pricing	○ ○	A B
○	○	26	Development of segmentation tools (e.g., sales tool)	○ ○	A B
	○	27	Prepare final report	○ ○	A B
	○	28	Deliver final recommendations	○	A B B B B B
	○	29	Discuss next steps	○	A B B
		A	OC Tanner Performance		
		B	PSKG Performance		

People working on the project: 10 10 10 10 4 4 4 4 10 10 10 10

Target Dates (Week ending): Jan-26, Feb-02, Feb-16, Mar-02, Mar-16, Mar-30, Apr-13, Apr-27, May-11, May-25, Jun-08, Jun-22

Owners: FL (PSKG), RK (PSKG), PSKG Team, CC (OCT), BT & Team, Other OCT Personnel

Left margin objectives: Create Tools / Conduct Research & Analysis / Logistics / Training / Plans

Diagram labels: Major Tasks — Target Dates (Week ending) — Objectives — Costs — Summary and Forecast

Phase 2: Actual $ / Budget $
Expenses: Actual $ / Budget $
□ Phase 2 ■ Expenses ■ = G □ = Y

Completed working session to determine key goals of segmentation project and main attributes.
Next steps: Develop a revised questionnaire to send to OC Tanner team by Feb 22. Schedule conference call to review draft the week of Feb 26.

FIGURE 7.2 *The Phase Two Consulting Report.*

who were working on the project. The last owner, PSKG Team, is a comparable team from the consulting firm. We arranged to have half the owners from our side (our lead and our team) and half from the consultant's side (their lead and their team) because this was such a collaborative effort. We absolutely needed the consultants to take ownership of some tasks, which is why they are on the OPPM.

This OPPM shows the project at its completion. All the tasks were completed on time. Note that Task 10, Recommend potential deal reconstruction candidates (which refers to taking all correspondence from a deal and reconstructing the process required from initial offer to final contract), has a square in the column for the week ending Nov. 03. We realized as the project progressed that this expanded task would take a week longer to complete than the two weeks originally allotted, so a square was inserted. When the task was completed, the square was filled in.

Take a look at Task 12: Exploratory interviews with internal stakeholders. The consultants interviewed managers, directors, and VPs of the company to get a collection of opinions about the strengths and weaknesses of our processes. This was done over two weeks (the weeks ending Oct. 27 and Nov. 03) and the circles have rectangular borders around them. The reason: We use the borders to delineate major milestones, tasks that must be completed for the project to move forward. Task 20, Deliver recommendations Dec. 6–7 also has a border around it for the same reason. These borders are placed around the squares at the beginning of the project so everyone who reads the OPPM knows which tasks are key. This major milestone heavy box may be used for significant critical path events or for any other reason requiring special focus or attention.

You will find an unusual line under the tasks, labeled # People working on the project. We wanted to keep track of how many of our people (this does not include consultants) were working on the project at any given time. These numbers are a head count and are not full-time equivalents.

One unique aspect of this OPPM can be found in the qualitative tasks. The consultant, who evaluates how well O.C. Tanner is performing, completes task A. Task B is completed by us to evaluate how the consultants are performing. When you do a project with a consultant, there is mutual dependency, and this fact needs to be communicated throughout the consultant's team and your project team. We did not reproduce this OPPM in color, but you probably will. Trust me, when everyone can see, in bright green, yellow and red, how the consultants are judging you (and you are judging the consultants), it tends to motivate performance. This is one way this OPPM is a management tool—our performance and the consultants' performance are clearly depicted.

The fact that the consultants are grading you is an incentive to your team and, of course, the consultants like it. The consultants graded us during two weeks (weeks ending Nov. 10 and Nov. 24) with yellow because information they needed to do their work was not received in a timely manner. We graded the consultants' performance yellow during the week ending Nov. 24 because they had challenges getting some of their methodology and tools to work properly. Notice that the last two weeks of the project are filled in with green, indicating both of these inadequacies were rectified.

Another unusual aspect of this OPPM comes under Costs. When dealing with consultants, frequently there are the consultants' professional fees, which are fixed, and then there are expenses, such as for hotels, travel, and photocopying. The chart shows bars and numbers to carefully track actual spending compared to budget. This is another way the tool is used to help manage the consultants. Having everyone looking at expenses helps control costs.

Proceeding to Phase 2 depended on the successful completion of Phase 1. Summary and Forecast noted that the first phase was successfully completed and that we were awaiting approval to begin Phase 2.

PHASE 2: ONE-PAGE PROJECT MANAGER

The next OPPM (Figure 7.2) shows Phase 2 three months into the project. I will not discuss every aspect of it, since it is similar to the OPPM we just discussed, but there are some differences, which are worth pointing out. Note that the Project Objective was expanded to read: Developing segment-specific offers to meet customer needs. This was done to explain how the focus of the project had gone from *creating* a strategy to *executing* the strategy.

The Major Tasks section is different than other OPPMs in that the tasks, which number 30, are divided into four sections shown in gray: Training Modules (Responsibility of TT), Survey Design (Responsibility of CC & DS), Survey Execution (Responsibility of CC & DS) and Survey Analysis (Responsibility of CC & DS). This was done to clearly delineate to the reader the four essential parts of the project. With this format, the reader can easily and quickly follow the project through its essential parts toward its conclusion. The gray areas are where we wanted to emphasize that there are three subparts to this project (design, execution, and analysis) all focused around the segment work. As with the OPPM for Phase 1, the qualitative tasks A and B have O.C. Tanner grading the consultants and the consultants grading O.C. Tanner.

As with the OPPM for Phase 1, this OPPM has major milestones delineated by boldly bracketed boxes. These include: Task 8, Finish questionnaire draft; Task 18, Delivery of final data from market research vendor; and Task 28, Deliver final recommendations.

The project's subobjectives (lower left-hand corner) are now: Create tools, conduct research and analysis, logistics/training/plans. These represent the new objectives of this phase.

The budget, as with Phase 1, is divided into professional fees and miscellaneous expenses. The expenses on this phase are so much higher than the first because they include the fees of a third vendor, a market research firm, which was to be secured by the consultant and paid out of these expenses.

These are the basics of Phase 2's OPPM.

Since many readers will deal with consultants during their careers, let me say a few words about these useful, though sometimes exasperating, outside vendors. Managing consultants brings with it a level of uncertainty combined with a mutual interdependence.

You hire a consultant to do something you cannot do yourself. By hiring them, you will eventually increase your own confidence in your ability to accomplish a new task, and you will increase your competence to deliver that task successfully; but not at first. The OPPM is a management and communication tool that makes it easier to tell each other how things are going and what is expected next.

The creation of the OPPM provides an essential meeting of the minds at the beginning of the consulting engagement. This tool, when dealing with a consulting project, is not just primarily aimed at an internal audience, but now includes, as a major goal, communicating to an external audience. You and the consultants come to a much clearer consensus on the project's scope, budget, and time line. And it facilitates a mutual commitment to meet those objectives. This is enormously valuable. The tool helps get a project off from the get-go with everyone reading from the same page (pun intended).

As with every OPPM, you also use the tool to communicate about the project to upper management.

By using the OPPM, we in effect consulted the consultants. They liked the OPPM so much, they bought copies of my first book, hired us to train them in its use, and then started using it themselves to manage their own projects world wide. The consultants found with the OPPM an important take-away that they now use to improve the performance of their projects and the communication with their clients.

Further, as in other types of projects, we found the status, steering, and other meetings we had with the consultants to be more efficient and effective than they would have been without the OPPM. This is another way in which the OPPM is a management as well as communication tool.

The OPPM is a profoundly valuable tool for managing consultants and communicating the essential elements of their work as a project progresses.

ISO 9000: Getting Certified

O.C. Tanner had the most advanced quality management systems in our industry. I'm not just saying that; we had statistics that backed up this claim. No question, we were the quality leader. But our competition had something we did not have, namely an ISO 9001:2000 certification. Even though our quality metrics exceeded our competitors, lacking this certification put us at a competitive disadvantage. We decided it would be prudent to secure an ISO 9001:2000 certification. Internally, we called the project ISO 9000—a kind of generic name for the type of certification we were seeking. ISO 9001:2000 is part of the family of the ISO 9000 certifications.

Strictly speaking, ISO 9000 certification is not an IT project. I included it in this book because it has a technical orientation and, in addition, ISO projects typically include IT processes.

ISO CERTIFICATION: WHAT IT IS

For those unfamiliar with ISO certifications, let me briefly explain them. The organization that oversees ISO certifications is the International Organization for Standardization, founded in 1947 and based in Geneva, Switzerland. ISO seeks to establish standards within industries that are benchmarks by which organizations can measure themselves. Typically, these standards are technically oriented.

There are various ISO standards. The two best known are ISO 9000 and ISO 14000, with the former addressing quality issues and the latter addressing environmental standards.

The ISO 9001:2000 certification includes procedures that cover a business' key processes and ways of monitoring and keeping track of these processes. It also includes standards for identifying product defects and strategies for eliminating such defects. According to ISO:

ISO 9000 is concerned with 'quality management.' This means what the organization does to enhance customer satisfaction by meeting customer and applicable regulatory requirements and continually to improve its performance in this regard.

About the ISO 9001: 2000 standard, which was established in the year 2000 and is now widely implemented, the ISO says: "ISO 9001:2000 is used if you are seeking to establish a management system that provides confidence in the conformance of your product to established or specified requirements." It includes, according to the ISO, five sections:

1. Activities used to supply your products,
2. Quality management systems,
3. Management responsibility,
4. Resource management and measurement, and
5. Analysis and improvement.

EARNING THE ISO CERTIFICATION

Obtaining certification is a complex, labor-intensive, time-consuming process. Each of our processes needed explicit quality objectives and documentation. In a general sense, we had to map out key processes and monitor and measure them, all with an eye toward assuring we were maintaining the desired level of quality. Even the quality of suppliers was addressed. And, as a company, we needed to determine the skill required for each and every job in our company, train each employee, and measure how effective that training was. Documenting procedures and results is a major part of ISO certification.

Getting certified is not easy or cheap. We already had implemented a number of programs based on the work of such management gurus as Joseph M. Juran, W. Edwards Deming, Philip Crosby, and Shigeo Shingo, as well as Lean Manufacturing. But as I noted, we needed to obtain this certification in order to communicate to the market our commitment to quality and our dedication to continuous quality improvement.

Marketing may have been the initial impetus, but an amplified culture of quality resulted from imbedding ISO diciplines. Let me also say on a more personal note that the quality orientation of ISO certification matched perfectly the philosophy of our company's founder, Obert C. Tanner, who died in 1993, after guiding the O.C. Tanner Company for 64 years. On a brass plaque in our headquarters, we have a quote from Obert: "We seek to touch the fringes of perfection." This became the slogan of our ISO project. ISO certification served to further improve our quality, and it helped us touch the fringes of perfection.

Let's look now at the One-Page Project Manager (OPPM) we created to manage this ISO project.

APPLYING THE ONE-PAGE PROJECT MANAGER

The ISO 9000 project did not require much customization of the standard OPPM (Figure 8.1). The standard elements included the objectives, which are listed in the bottom left corner of the form. Note the first objective is Organizational Commitment. This refers to the commitment of the organization toward obtaining the ISO certification. Of course, all projects require a strong commitment from the organization. But with a project like ISO certification, the absolute commitment of everyone in the organization, including management, is absolutely essential, which is why we made it one of our objectives. Without such commitment, it is easy for other, seemingly more pressing business issues to take priority.

Project Leader: Larry Hamilton	Project: ISO 9000		Date: Sept 30
Project Objective: Achieve ISO 9001:2000 Certificaton			

Objectives	Major Tasks	Project Completed By: Feb	Owner/Priority
	Definition Phase		
●	1 Establish Development Team	● ●	A B
●	2 Train Development Team	● ●	A B B
●	3 Develop Process Map	● ●	B A
●	4 Select Registrar	● ●	B A
● ● ●	5 Define Level II Procedures	● ● ●	A B B
● ● ●	6 Quality Manual	● ● ● ●	B B B A
● ● ●	7 Work Instructions and Forms	● ● ● ●	A B
● ● ● ●	8 Records	● ● ● ●	A
	Implementation Phase		
● ● ● ●	9 Train New Processes	● ●	B A A
●	10 Publish Quality Manual	● ● ●	A
●	11 New Forms/Work Instructions		A B
● ●	12 Put Procedures under Document Control	● ●	A B B
●	13 Implement Procedures	● ● ●	A B B
○ ○ ○ ○ ○	14 Awareness Training	● ● ○	B A
	Verification Phase		
●	15 Develop and Train Internal Auditors	● ●	B A
● ●	16 Implement Internal Auditing Program	● ●	B B A B
● ● ● ● ●	17 Conduct Management Review	● ●	A B B
● ● ● ●	18 Conduct Pre-Audit Assessment	● ●	B A
○	19 Pre-Audit Corrective Actions	○ ○	B A B
	Validation Phase		
○ ○ ○ ○ ○	20 Registration Audit	● ○	A B
○ ○ ○ ○	21 Corrective Actions	○ ○ ○	B A
○	22 Certification	○ ○	A A A A A
○	23 Project Closeout	○ ○	A B B B
●	A Organizational Commitment		A B B B
○ ○ ○ ○ ○ ○	B Our Performance		B A B B
○ ○ ○ ○ ○ ○	C Consultant Performance		B B B B A

# Procedures Completed:	1/17	6/17	12/17	17/20	17/19	19/19

Objectives: Organizational Commitment · Develop Quality Manual · Develop Procedures · Develop Work Instructions · Develop Records · Develop Internal Audit System

Major Tasks / Target Dates

Target Dates: April · May · June · July · August · September · October · November · December · January · February

Owner/Priority: Executive Management · Project Manager · ISO Project Teams · Internal Auditors · ISO Consultant

Costs and Metrics

Summary and Forecast

Expenses 135 / 150 ☐ Expended ☐ Budgeted
Work Instructions 580 / 580
Records 307 / 307
■ Completed ☐ Required ■ = G ☐ = Y

FIGURE 8.1 *The September ISO 9000 Report.*

ISO certification is easy to place on the back burner, and when that happens, it is unlikely the organization will ever get the certification it wants. We also list organizational commitment under Major Tasks (Task A).

As I mentioned, written materials and processes are a very important part of the ISO certification process. The remaining objectives, including Develop Quality Manuals, Develop Procedures, Develop Work Instructions, Develop Records, and Develop Internal Audit System address these needs.

Phases of the Project

One aspect of this project that is somewhat unusual is our breaking it down into four phases. We delineated the phases on the tool with horizontal gray lines, each labeled with a phase: Definition Phase, Implementation Phase, Verification Phase, and Validation Phase. These phases represent an often used standard methodology for ISO implementation projects, helping the project team break the project down into manageable chunks it could more easily focus on. These phases are comprised of 23 quantitative tasks (1 through 23) and three qualitative tasks (A through C).

As an indication of the complexity of this project, most of these tasks had their own OPPM, such as Task 6, Quality Manual. Creating this manual was a significant project by itself. Some tasks, such as Task 14, Awareness Training, did not require a full OPPM. Here, the trainer had on her desk a simple task list that consisted of who was to be trained and when. But many of the other tasks were sufficiently large and complex that they needed to be broken down more granularly into additional owners, objectives, and time lines.

One strength of the OPPM is that it can be used to drill down further and further when necessary, making even the most complex project suitable for the OPPM.

On the qualitative side, Tasks A (Organizational Commitment), B (Our Performance) and C (Consultant Performance) were so critical that we wanted to track each of these with a color line throughout the project. As we talked about in a previous chapter, with projects where you engage the services of a consultant, it is very helpful to include a place on the OPPM where the consultant gives you a score and you give the consultant a score. That's what we've done here with Task B (Our Performance) and Task C (Consultant's Performance). It is a powerful incentive to keep our consultant and us on task by having our performance and the consultant's on public display via the OPPM.

On the right-hand side of the form, we have Owner/Priority. We broke the owners into five groups: Executive Management, Project Manager, ISO Project Teams, Internal Auditors, and ISO Consultant. I've said elsewhere that we don't usually have someone outside of the company as an owner. In this situation, we made an exception by making the consultant an owner for four of the major tasks. We did this because the consultant played a very important role relating to certain tasks; it made sense to designate him as an owner. For example, Task 3, Develop Process Map, has the consultant as the top priority owner. That's because we did not know how to do this task while the consultant did, and therefore, the primary responsibility for completing this task fell to the consultant. There are few absolutes in the use of the OPPM. It is highly flexible. The project is the important thing. The OPPM is for the project; the project is not for the OPPM.

The time line (the horizontal line near the bottom labeled Target Dates) shows the length of the project (11 months) and the frequency of the reporting periods (monthly). Choosing monthly time buckets for the reporting period was arbitrary. We could have divided the time into biweekly periods, for example, but felt that monthly reporting was sufficiently frequent to keep the project on track and not so frequent as to make the reporting too time consuming. Progress on the ISO 9000 project was reported monthly to the full management staff using the OPPM as the principal PowerPoint slide.

A critical, absolutely essential element of ISO 9000 is the identification and documentation of procedures. The number of these procedures is determined as you go through the project and can change over time. The procedures have to be thoroughly documented and accompanied with work instructions and records. We tracked this documentation on the OPPM in two ways. One was under the various tasks.

But the second way is unique to this OPPM. You see it on the line directly above the Target Dates section labeled #Procedures Completed. In April, we thought we needed 17 procedures and one had been thoroughly documented and completed (which is why the April box has 1/17 in it). By July, we had documented 17 procedures but reasoned we needed three more (17/20), which means we had added three procedures to the 17 we had originally. But by September, we figured we needed only 19 procedures and that all had been completed (19/19).

Also, as mentioned previously, we use bold squares to highlight major milestones. This OPPM has three such squares. The first was Task 18, Conduct Pre-Audit Assessment. It was to be completed in September, which is noted in the bold square indicating this date. This task, as shown on the form, was completed on time. The second milestone was Task 20, Registration Audit, which is to be completed by November. And the third was Task 22, Certification, which is to be completed by January. These were the three most critical tasks in the project.

Another variation of the standard OPPM found with this form is the cost section, which has been expanded to read Costs and Metrics. The first bar, Expenses, shows we have spent $135,000 out of a budgeted $150,000. It is yellow because we are running a little over budget.

You will see that this section also includes Work Instructions and Records. These are the supporting building blocks and metrics needed for the procedures. There were 19 procedures in our company, under which there were 580 work instructions. There can be one procedure that requires 100 work instructions, for instance, while another procedure that requires only one or two. The records document the processes. One value of the OPPM with a project as complex as ISO 9000 is that anyone with this tool can assess the progress of the project with one look.

Speaking of how well the OPPM relates the progress of the project, note that at the time of this OPPM, two tasks were behind schedule and one ahead of schedule. Task 14, Awareness Training, should have been completed in August, but we are now in September and it has yet to be completed. Task 19, the Pre-Audit Corrective Actions, did not start in September, as planned. Task 20, the Registration Audit, has started early and what was scheduled to be completed in October has been completed in September.

Also worth noting is Task A, which has been strong throughout the project. But Tasks B and C have not been as consistent. Our performance slipped in June and July when scheduled vacations slowed the project more than anticipated. We recovered in August. The consultant fell behind in July and August, but recovered and is on track in September.

These are the major elements in this ISO 9000 OPPM. This project, though complex, did not require much customization of the OPPM. In one page, with very little variation from the standard format, we were able to convey all the important information upper management would need to know about this project.

As a postscript, O.C. Tanner was certified ISO 9000 compliant on schedule. The auditors' conclusion was that O.C. Tanner's system was not only ISO compliant but was unusually mature and substantially more robust than the typical first-time applicant.

Customizing the One-Page Project Manager

One of the strengths of the One-Page Project Manager (OPPM) is that it can readily be customized to meet virtually every high-level communication need of the project manager. As you have seen in this book, the tool can take many forms to fit the shapes and variables of many types of projects. Yet, there is also a consistency to the variations that make the tool immediately identifiable as an OPPM. But if customization is not properly managed, it can become one of the tool's great weaknesses.

Consistency and simplicity are absolutely vital. It is good to customize if needed, but it is very bad to customize too much. Changing the basic template by too great an extent lessens the tool's value. That's because the greater the difference between the OPPMs that you use, the more difficult it is for the tool to communicate. The power of the tool is that anyone familiar with it can immediately read it and glean the important information it contains. This is very powerful for the project manager who is trying to communicate with others. The more the template is changed, the less familiar is the tool to the reader, resulting in the reader having to work much harder to learn what the OPPM is saying. It is possible to make the OPPM so customized and complex, that it can no longer adequately communicate the information it was designed to communicate.

THE INVIOLATE RULES OF THE ONE-PAGE PROJECT MANAGER

Because it is tempting for inexperienced project managers to customize the OPPM too much, I have created a series of inviolate rules that must be followed. Break these rules at your own peril:

1. The OPPM is so-called because it must be on one page. Period. Never create an OPPM that violates the tool's name.

2. The five elements of every project must be clearly delineated on the OPPM. These elements are: Tasks, Time Line, Owners, Objectives, and Costs. All five elements must be on every OPPM. Depending on the project, you may have additional elements, but these five must always be there.

3. The aligning element of the OPPM, the Matrix—which is on the lower-left hand corner—must be included

in every OPPM. It is critical because it displays the five essential elements of every project and every OPPM (see Rule 2, above), and because it provides a context for the alignment of these elements.

4. Standard symbols must be used. Always use an empty circle for a planned task and a filled circle to indicate a completed task. An empty square is to be used when a task is longer than planned and, when the task is completed, the square is filled in. It's a matter of judgment whether a task is considered to be going longer than planned or is just plain late. If the task is simply going to be late, don't use a square. On the other hand, if the scope of the task has increased (the insidious scope creep), it is acceptable to add squares.

5. Always use red, yellow, and green. Period. Using other colors just confuses things.

6. Quantitative and qualitative tasks are always kept separate. The former is shown with dots, while the latter is reported with colors, as in the bar graphs used to depict the budget. Do not use colors with dots or dots in the colors.

7. The header needs to clearly state the name of the project, the name of the project manager, and the objective of the project. The header does not change during the project, which makes it very important that it be used, accurate, and complete. The information it contains will be used to identify the project throughout its history—and even after the project is completed.

8. The space for the Summary and Forecast must be kept small. The OPPM is primarily a graphic communication tool. Too many words weaken its power to communicate. The larger the space available for the Summary and Forecast, the greater the temptation will be to write and explain things. This tendency must be controlled, and a small space is a wonderful control mechanism.

TYPES OF CUSTOMIZATION

I divide customization into two types, simple and advanced.

Simple

In the simple type of customization, you change only the basic variables. These include: the number and length of the time buckets, the types of costs to be budgeted and tracked, the types and number of quantitative and qualitative tasks, the types and number of objectives, and the number of owners and who they are.

Here are some rules governing these basic variables:

- The number of tasks should be about three times the number of time buckets. If you have a six-month project, for example, and you divided the project into six, monthly time buckets, you should have about 18 tasks.
- The number of subobjectives should be three to six. Three is better.
- The number of owners should be manageable—not too few and not too many. Leave this to the judgment of the project manager.

All of these can be easily accommodated with Microsoft Excel by increasing and decreasing the number of rows and columns and by using specific symbols.

Advanced

For an example of an advanced OPPM, look at the one we discussed earlier for the Recognition@work dot-com project. This is a complex OPPM and I do not recommend you create such a version the first time you use the tool. With this project, the standard OPPM was reduced to the lower half of the page and consolidated. On the top, charts, tables, and other scorecards were added. Graphics were included to show performance, and the RACI model was incorporated.

Advanced customization should be rare and used only when it significantly increases one or more of the following three objectives:

1. To better communicate what you want your stakeholders to *know*.
2. To better communicate how you hope the project team members will *feel*, that is, their ownership and motivation.
3. To more clearly communicate what you are *doing*.

As you add more charts, graphs, tables, and unique elements to the standard OPPM format, you make the report less a project management tool and more a customized scorecard.

I estimate 90-plus percent of all projects can be adequately represented on an OPPM using the standard format and symbols and basic customization. You can find a collection of OPPM formats at www .onepageprojectmanager.com. We encourage readers to add their own OPPMs so this database continually expands.

You'll also find that as you use the tool, you will be able to increasingly represent complex projects using the standard format and basic customization. It is worth trying hard to do this, rather than looking for ways to customize the form. The OPPM's ability to communicate is a direct function of its simplicity and consistency. Simplicity and consistency should be your goals. You will be tempted as a project manager who knows a project better than anyone else to overcomplicate the tool. Resist this temptation! I have seen plenty of examples of OPPMs that became so complex; they were eventually discarded and not used. The more complex the OPPM, the more difficult it is to report the project's status as it progresses.

The simpler you make your OPPM, the more successful will be the deployment of your project and the communication of your project's essential information. As a successful project manager, you are, by your very nature, detail oriented. That concentration on details has long been an important contributor to your success. You follow up on things; you readily chart, graph, and measure; you love details—which is why you have to fight your own inclination to be complex.

Initially, it will feel counterintuitive to keep the OPPM as simple and consistent as possible but trust me, the simpler the tool, the more successful will be your project.

Clark Addison Campbell is the award winning author of the highly acclaimed book, *The One-Page Project Manager.* He has advised corporations and taught university graduate students the power and simplicity of "OPPM" in the United States and China.

As Senior Vice President at O.C. Tanner, he leads the Professional Services Division. Tanner is a world leader in recognition solutions—enabling clients to meet their objectives by powering appreciation to communicate their message. Clark also directs Tanner's Project Management Office. He held planning and project management responsibilities at the DuPont Chemical Company prior to joining O.C. Tanner.

Clark is a University of Utah alumnus, with a BS in Chemical Engineering and an MBA. He and his wife Meredith (violinist and recording artist) live in Salt Lake City, Utah, and are the parents of seven children and eight grandchildren.